TOUGH LOVE

Noga Sklar

TOUGH LOVE

1st Edition
POD

KBR
Greenville
2017

Cover design **KBR**

Title in Portuguese: *Amor, duro amor*
Copyright © 2017 *Noga Sklar*
All rights reserved.

ISBN Paperback: 978-1-944608-55-2
ISBN E-Book: 978-1-944608-54-5
Library of Congress Control Number: 2017904666

KBR Digital Publishers LLC.
www.kbrdigital.com
www.facebook.com/kbrdigital
contact@kbrdigital.com

Greenville - SC
1|864|373.4528

LCO019000 — Essays/ Women authors

To my husband Alan, a master of tough love.

Forgive me my nonsense, as I also forgive the nonsense of those who think they talk sense.

Robert Frost

TABLE OF CONTENTS

American Poverty

"**I**n America, the poor drive cars," Alan told me some ten years ago, when we first met on the Internet. It was kind of a dream thing, which might include a golden Mercedes, like the one we've bought for only five thousand dollars and have been driving for over a year, without any hassle so far. Based on the minimum wage I will describe below, this car costs only two months of American labor; translated into Brazilian reality, two months of the average wage would amount to 1,500 *Brazilian reals*.

Now, is this still true?

According to U.S. presidential candidates on "both sides of the aisle," the answer is "not at all."

"Americans are getting poorer," they say. "And for the first time in recent history we will not leave our children a better country than the one we live in." Despite the candidates' fierce differences in political ideology, the complaint is unanimous, with very few variations.

The thing is, "poverty" here in the U.S. is a salary of $25,000 — a hundred thousand *reals* in our precious Brazilian currency. Democrats candidates are "fighting" for a "minimum wage" of $15 an hour, amounting to about $600 a week, $2,400 per month — almost 10,000 *reals* in our precious currency. That is, if you consider an eight-hour day in a five-day week, which, let's face it, nobody can afford anymore. Take me, for example: as a highly-specialized editor and a qualified graphic designer, I work around 12 hours a day, seven days a week. And I won't even tell you how much my hourly rate is, but I can tell you this: If it wasn't for the love of the craft, I would be opting to clean houses, although in this regard I couldn't offer the same "expertise" as my cleaning lady from Venezuela, who is relatively incompetent, by the way. At 25 bucks an hour.

Okay. One cannot always take into account the absurd dollar to *real* exchange rate; and if it is true that there is "no fun left for those who convert the currency," imagine a person who works in two such diverse countries simultaneously. It's insane.

I'm full of hope with my new plans for an international KBR, a hope that has increased greatly since I found a local associate who shares with me the same love for world literature, the same lack of hesitation when it comes to exhausting work hours (whatever the currency), and the same chutzpah to pursue every chance she sees. Much like myself, but with the appropriate accent, get it?

The only downside is that KBR's original "business model" had to be significantly altered, and I confess that I'm having a hard time trying to fit into the new "shape" presented by this capitalist market. Within my innate "Gestalt," borrowing money is a non-bailable crime, but in a truly capitalist economy... Well, I must confess that I don't know how to operate within a subsidized interest rate, which oscillates between 0 and 3%... A year!

Meanwhile, in my beloved Brazil, recent developments keep confirming an old adage that equates lawful entrepreneurs with stupid entrepreneurs, those who will never, ever make any money, regardless of talent or ability, as long as they insist on this silliness of being honest. Tough stuff. One by one, the big "tycoons" are falling behind bars, as they reveal their favorite little governmental schemes in their plea bargains — Worker's Party style, if you please.

Back to the U.S. (I resisted typing "U.S.S.A.," as in "United Socialist States of America"): One of the most successful presidential candidates in this country is a "leftist" who's promising the world to people, lots of free fish and fewer and fewer fishing lessons. Which is the perfect recipe for the winning of votes and the bankruptcy of the National Treasury. Whoever doubts its effectiveness can ask our dearest President Dilma back home. On the other hand, I've begun to wonder how this "bag of goodness" would work here in the U.S., with the poverty level up to 25,000. Dollars, of course.

Bear with me for a moment: I believe more and more in that saying that claims "if you're not a liberal at twenty, you have no heart, but if you're not a conservative at forty, you have no brain," Arnaldo Jabor will have to forgive me. (It never hurts to remember that Jabor, a famous Brazilian writer, columnist, and movie director, still holds a grudge against the United States from being traumatized as a teenager, during his stay in Florida in the 1950s, when, according to his claims, he was bullied by the children of "the conservative bigwigs.")

I'm getting old, my friends. And I trust more and more my brain and its careful considerations, and less and less the "miracle of multiplication." I don't wish to sound mean at all, but I still believe that the best way to ensure one's survival is through dedication and hard work, and that everybody must do their share the best they can, despite all insistent evidence to the contrary.

I know. I'll never learn.

If all else fails, or as old age advances, then it might be acceptable to consider some help from the government. But not for me; God forbid I would ever rely on some social safety net. It would be too humiliating, please spare me the pain. Hopefully, in the few years that I have left, I'll learn my way around in the world of a strong capitalist economy (which, I hope, American voters will keep that way, rooted in the foundation of capital abundance), paving a path to produce my own nest egg. With my eggs in different baskets, of course.

Let me remind you that, despite Obama's idealism — which in the past I endorsed so open-heartedly, without reservation — the truth is that I haven't seen the world improve one iota during the nearly eight years of his presidency, quite the opposite.

I'm not sure right-wing radicalism is the best way either, not at all. I see Donald Trump's rhetoric as excessive, filled with dangerously misconceived ideas. But this does not stop me from concluding that pretending not to see what our increasingly terrible enemies are doing, and refusing to acknowledge the fact that a government policy of "racial equality" has resulted in the most dangerous climate of violence and division in recent years, didn't work very well.

Think it's bad with Obama? It will be far worse with Hillary.

And that's what I had to say.

Hope

I know. Judging by what I've been writing lately (and, therefore, thinking — or is it the other way around?) my main concern in recent times has been about… money; but, wait a minute. In recent times? Wasn't it always like this?

Today, I'm in fairly good health, it is true; and if, a long time ago, I was forced to overcome big and painful dramas that forged my slightly bipolar persona, I no longer deal with these problems on a daily basis. This, however, does not make it any easier to become a bestselling author in the highly-disputed life-changing calamities market.

Nonetheless, the reduced number of problems makes me at least halfway happy, let me explain. Although this topic touches on one of my greatest frustrations, I'd obviously rather enjoy a quiet maturity than keep on bleeding until the end, if you know what I mean.

Just one year ago, I thought I had found some sort of "perfect life project": Alan and I would leave Brazil for the U.S., where we would build a house on the property we had chosen, and then pursue the type of retirement plan that you don't need to pay back, the famous "reverse mortgage." The mortgage lender evaluates your home, gives you half of the appraised value in cash, and when you die, there's some kind of payment arrangement. I'm not sure what it's like, but by then I'll be dead. Why should I care, right?

I would never be forced to work again. No more troubled nights, weekends lost to solving endless problems or editing the most complex of theses, to tracking elaborate printing processes in Brazil from afar; or, speaking as an "author," to the inevitable fear of being rejected. All this would be left behind. We would travel at will, Alan and I, to distant and exotic destinations, no further delay, nothing else to get in our way. Everything would rhyme beautifully.

As I write this bunch of crap destined to never come true, I can hear the annoying noise of the leaf blower outside. Then I think of Brazil, of the Serenity Valley we left behind... Our neighborhood administrator back there had tried to "please" us... by deciding to use a leaf blower that tortured us and the rest of the local residents every damn morning. Now, looking out the window, I can finally understand how useful a leaf blower really is... a tool that makes a lot of sense, indeed, at least in this Northern Hemisphere autumn. We had had 10 days of rain, and countless fallen leaves were scattered everywhere, leaving an impression of messiness and abandonment; now they are neatly arranged on small mounds that will soon be vacuumed up by the leaf truck, restoring cleanliness and order. Now, in our tropical Brazil, how many leaves really fall each year?

Oh well. It's not the first time I've thought about Brazil since I woke up today. Imagine that, when I opened the computer this morning, I've got an email containing this month's electricity bill, an absurd $144, considering that we haven't been using the air conditioning, nor the heating, and last month's bill had fallen to about $70... The comparison was intriguing, to say the least. I prepared myself to complain, despite feeling relieved for not having to deal with the scandalous 50% increase recently faced by my friends in Brazil, not to mention the shortage of water, the endless heat wave, the smothering of political scandals, and the precarious situation of the Minister of Finance... Tough stuff. I should be content that I'm safe from all these woes, but nothing justifies this highly expensive electricity bill, right?

Yes. I still indulge in our old Brazilian disgust. Nevertheless, when I accessed the website... I found out that, in fact, we didn't have to pay any bill. On the contrary, the company owed us! Apparently (I had already erased these records from my head), a year ago, when we registered with the power company, we had made a $200 deposit that is now being returned, *et voilà*. We will enjoy about three months of "free" energy, *ooh la la*.

The whole episode reminded me of the compulsory deposits in Brazil, the "kidnapping" of our savings accounts, and other "mandatory" loans to previous federal governments, accompanied by the worrisome uncertainty as to whether we would ever recover these resources. Ouch. Better not mention any of that. Imagine if our dearest President Dilma decides it's a good idea, a valuable strategy to save her sorry ass... God forbid, such a bad omen; when it rains, it pours, as my mom would say.

These unhappy memories, I must admit, almost made me drop the main subject, but now I'm resuming it: While I was toting around the idea of my unprecedented retirement plan (right, I used to say that artists never retire, as they work for sheer pleasure, entertaining the idea of dying while working; but never before in this harsh existence have I ever felt so tired, needing break after break), a year went by and my credit improved. The house we were planning to build, however, did not show any sign of getting off the paper, until... life reconfigured itself, and the hopes of an extended break sponsored by the bank ended up turning into a new publishing enterprise, as per U.S. rules, this time.

Therefore, here I am again, getting ready to work until I die. And with a lot of pleasure. But this time, I hope — as the wishes of those who hope will always be granted, at least according to the American dream — without having to kill myself from too much work, as I have done in recent years.

Now, concerning my worries about money, this too shall pass. Imagine that a year ago, when I arrived in the U.S., I had to accept being a "second-rate" citizen — no credit, no permanent residence, solely dependent on my own resilience. Today, I happily carry a Green Card (even if, assuming I understood correctly from watching the Republican debate, the majority of immigrants don't give a damn), and I just received in the mail a credit card offer that will probably restore my mileage credit, which we often used in the past to travel abroad and was left behind in Brazil as well. My request to move the credit up here had been denied a few months ago; I had already forgotten the whole issue, but the "system" remembered, figure that.

That's right. Time heals everything. What it does not mend, ends up falling into oblivion, which is one of our brain's greatest qualities, perhaps the final key to the door to happiness. I've even made peace with my failed "apartment herb garden," where my basil keeps dying no matter what. It must be the fall, that's all.

As for our house in Paris Mountain, we'll keep on waiting. Sooner than expected, the construction will get off the ground. I'll make sure to let you know.

LA HAINE

My weekly chronicle was already ready in two languages when I went out to run a few errands on my day off, have a drink with Alan, relax, go to the supermarket. Then we got back home, and as Alan turned on the TV, my subject matter died right there, on the spot. An "incident" had taken place in Paris.

A few noises. Shots. An explosion.

No one really knew what was going on.

About two hours later, the events' pictures seemed to have evolved a bit. As I write, I listen to live TV in the background. A suspect has been arrested by the police.

"I'm from Syria. I was recruited by ISIS. This is an ISIS mission."

There are 100 hostages held at this moment at Café Bataclan, where self-indulgence was practiced freely, people danced, an American band was giving a concert. Thirty people are dead. No one knows anything else.

"*Allahu akbar!*"

This war cry was unnecessary, in all honesty.

Despite the complete misinformation about what is

occurring, the French borders are closed right now. Nobody comes in, nobody goes out.

There are six locations in Paris being attacked simultaneously by terrorists (I am now reviewing this text; while I was writing it, nobody knew that those animals had attacked Les Halles, the "Parisian World Trade Center"). For the first time since 1944, Paris is in lock-down. Under siege. The second major location is the Stade de France, where there was a soccer match being played between Germany and France, and President Hollande was present.

The police have controlled the situation at the Bataclan.

The horror is being reported live in the background, while this chronicle is being written live.

Yes. The horror.

The world is lucky — or unlucky, I'm not sure — that the hatred I feel cannot contaminate world leaders, at least not in the open.

I want my life back. What about you?

So, here's my plan. And it's not xenophobic, as the "good guys" have already begun to declare on social networks. It's only logical, based on the facts. We're at war; and this is a cruel war, much aggravated because it's not located in a given place, also aggravated by the fact that the enemy is not motivated by national pride, nor by a deplorable, albeit explicable, national trauma, but by an irrational hatred.

There was no doubt, even from the first moment, that this orchestrated attack was triggered by Islamic terrorism. No one dares to declare it yet, but this is the (not so simple) truth. Everything is "in process." Nobody knows what will come next, but a specific certainty underlines all the comments and reports: This is another attack on civilization, on human values, on love, freedom, joy, on the enjoyment of technology, and on so many other things it would take me all night to enumerate them.

Again, here's my plan. Hate me if you will, if it alleviates your consciousness, but if something is not done immediately, things will just tend to get worse, and soon none of us in the "civilized" world will have anywhere to turn to. Life on the planet as we know it will be over, and that terrible scenario of sci-fi films will prevail. Yes, those films I detest and refuse to watch.

One hundred and forty dead right now (the number is in flux).

Islamic terrorism must be wiped out from the face of the Earth. Extremist Islamic countries must be declared our enemies. External signs of praise of Islam must be discouraged, charming *keffiyehs* confined to the drawers. I'm hiding mine, the red one I've always loved and wore proudly for so many years. I was 20 years old when I bought it, living in Israel, in the period between the Six-Day War and the Yom Kippur War.

Any connection with a Muslim background must be thoroughly vetted, scrutinized. Yes, innocent people will suffer. Innocent people suffered in the Inquisition as well; at that time, persecution had no other basis than religious hatred, it is true. It was motivated by the same kind of loyalty to some insane, blood-thirsty god, which needs to be eradicated right away, and still, Islamic ties must be denounced.

Innocents must suffer. Better them than me, or you.

Good Muslims, please understand the gravity of the situation. There was not a second of doubt, from the first blast, that this heinous attack had come from Islamic extremists, and soon enough the jihad cry was uttered: "*Allahu akbar!*"

We are all suffering deeply.

The evil nature of this war plan, essentially a global defense plan, will not start with us, Westerners, attacked in the intimacy of our everyday lives, in which we hate nobody, condemn no one. Contrary to our inhumane enemies, we do not base our actions on a code of faith that stopped evolving in the 16th century, on an ideological blindness that takes any victims it can. The evil nature of this plan of war comes from the group itself we're about to attack. Years have passed, during which the situation grew increasingly serious, and no one in these despicable bastards' countries of origin ever rejected them, condemned them publicly, decided to lock them up in some kind of human zoo, like they deserved. I'm sorry. I must apologize to animals, actually, as my comparison might hurt them deeply; yet, this is the metaphor that comes to mind.

Yes. I apologize to the wolves, to the dogs, to the snakes, and even to the rats, and cockroaches of this world, because to call such terrorists "animals" is offensive to them, to the whole animal kingdom: When animals carry out their violent instincts, they do so solely to ensure survival; they do not tear their victims to pieces in the name of a dead god and his prophet, who is also long dead. Kill me if you like.

Ironically, the film that gives its name to this chronicle depicted the sad lives of French immigrants in the suburbs of Paris, in the 1990s. The hatred we witness today is the other side of that same coin, but also the one and only face of it, just going through another phase, since nothing has been done to improve the situation. Moreover, nobody in their right mind could imagine back then where all this hatred would take us, a violence beyond imagination.

Innocent people, all of them.

Except those who penetrate softly into the "enemy camp," under the mask of refugees, persecution victims, under the blessings of envoys of goodness, disseminators of kindness active in social networks, convinced that they're doing their best in defense of humanity. But they are wrong. They are mistaken, deluded. They are co-opted, and don't even seem to know it.

I hate them. I hate them. I hate them. My hate today is equivalent to theirs, to the hatred of those who attack us. But this does not mean I'll go into the streets covered in explosives and take with me, in my irrationality, people who have nothing to do with my beliefs. No, I confine myself to the violence of these words, mainly because, beneath the terror perpetrated by these demons (I had written "animals," but changed it as I proof-read it), there's nothing more than that: words. Words written long ago and horribly misinterpreted today.   W o r d s uttered today by someone who claims to be a prophet, an emissary of some god, but who nonetheless, is no more than human trash.

A last remark: A Facebook friend placed a comment to a picture posted on my wall, subtitled "*J'aime Paris*," saying that "I'd better love Israel, because this attack and any other coming from Muslims is ultimately against Israel." I could not agree more. I find it unbelievable that minutes after I called my friends' attention to a subtle connection among my most recent Facebook posts, most of them about the anti-Israel stupidity of the Brazilian singer Caetano Veloso, this same connection has been displayed with absolute clarity in the Paris attacks. Hatred is in the air.

***

The Monday after: it never hurts to clarify that this chronicle was written on Friday night, under the heat of the attacks, and therefore it does not express reflective thoughts nor a mature conclusion. Some of the positions I've taken may sound offensive indeed, but I decided to keep them in order to let the heart talk, the first impression prevail, with transparency. I did not want to risk the obvious confusion faced by most people who were interviewed on TV these past few days, as was the case with a French Senator interviewed by CNN. While trying to express herself as "not xenophobic" and politically correct, she ended up contradicting herself every 2 minutes. She sounded insane, unable to meld a mere two thoughts into a coherent statement.

CHAOS AND CONFUSION

When you decide to dedicate your life to writing, planning to be read by others, one of the first pieces of advice you'll likely hear is that you should "write about what you know."

It makes sense. If there's something anyone can understand, it is the personal stuff we go through, which, in time, becomes our own "life experience." Right?

The best, the deepest philosophy is one that is based upon reflections on life itself, or on the life led by each one of us. It is expected that the quality of the result, whether by cause or consequence I'm not sure, will reflect the intelligence, knowledge and sensitivity of the one who writes it, ideally inciting understanding in those who read it. A good start.

At any rate, today these simple rules are as obsolete as the fact that, in the past, people were born and raised (and often died) without setting foot outside of their hometown, where everyone knew everyone else. Instructions were clear and direct, and when added to a small arsenal of accumulated human knowledge, provided the certainty of a quiet life within the family realm. Few dared to extrapolate beyond this limit, since things "out there" always entailed considerable risk: the risk of adventure; the risk of success, or failure; the risk of the unknown; and also, the risk of an utterly unknown, yet coveted happiness.

The lure of the unknown was, at that time, the reason, the driving force behind the expansion of knowledge. Each framework of ideas had its own natural maturation time, and if time proved the value of these considerations, they could be published in a book, and added to the scope of existing ideas. *Et voilà*, we were back to the starting point, but with human culture made a little richer.

It was a world in which people knew little, but this little was well known, mostly without the painful awareness of how limited that knowledge was.

Outside of this peaceful everyday existence, lived the great leaders and their heroic subordinates, whose daily lives were spent in war; from time to time, they would come home for a "family holiday," that is, if they were still alive. Now and then, one expected that a tragedy would occur, due to some dramatic weak spot in the village defense. Invasion, death and destruction would follow.

Nothing and no one was arguably good, or unquestionably bad. Everything was relative, changing according to the conditions and the people who put themselves in leadership positions. The others adapted the best they could.

There was night. There was day. God had set them apart a long time ago, the book told us, starting a movement of constant evolution, improvement, enhanced civilization. Above all that, hovered an even greater certainty, engaging, all-encompassing, capable of explaining all future uncertainty: The faith in a divine being who loved us and protected us, and who knew everything there was to know; and who, under the right circumstances, would occasionally share his knowledge with us. Everything we could not explain through our rational views could be surely explained by our spiritual views.

This ancient perspective has little or nothing to do with our world today, in which we are often forced to live by rules we are not aware of, and worse, changing on a daily basis. And here we are. The borders of the communities in which we live have dissolved into virtual reality, transforming the world into the much celebrated "global village." A village in which, however, regardless of the most idealistic predictions, we are not all brothers and sisters; on the contrary, we are all foreigners, becoming more estranged every day, our predictable lives increasingly plunged into chaos and confusion, all of us talking at the same time with little knowledge of what we say, or intend to say. We may communicate in a common language, but it is one that, unfortunately, nobody really understands. We are all trying to conduct ourselves according to the highest, most advanced parameters, in step with modern slogans broadcast in real time by the news channels — continuously, day and night — trying to act based on hashtags created just the day before or the latest tweets we read. In this unprecedentedly competitive environment, we seek to express the most elevated feelings, and follow the most highly exacerbated mores of perfect humanism. And that, more often than not, ends up in situations that are the exact opposite of our initial intentions.

There is an ongoing, widely spread disagreement. Could this be proof that the future is in fact the past? Might the universe be shrinking, collapsing back into the state in which it had begun?

Considering the terrible recent events, why did I

suddenly choose to take refuge in such deep thoughts, so radically distinct from actual events?

At first, I admit, I could not find an effective way to express my gut feelings in writing. These were of hatred, revolt, impediment, so close to my heart and yet terribly estranged. I had the displeasure of seeing my chronicle about the Paris attacks — which I had written almost blindly, in the darkness of early developments, my mind stumbling in a liquid that felt like lukewarm water, but was, in fact, the blood being shed — be censored by a major news portal under the claim that it contained "offensive and dangerous" material.

Offensive and dangerous? Me? I was shocked.

Make no mistake, as did the Internet robot that blocked me. It was just an "unfortunate" choice of words, "unfortunate," of course, according to current evaluation parameters, because in this world today many written words are read out of context, apart, therefore, from their original, true meaning. Sometimes they are confused by some random filter of most utilized lexicon in such a way that their honest purpose can be easily manipulated.

Much has been said and shared recently as mere lip service, controlled by the unidentified rules of an ongoing ideological totalitarianism, although they may sound straightforward, open, said from the heart. And this would include me. Everything seems to contradict the desired direction. Knowledge, which was once seen as sin, the reason why we were expelled from the paradise of not-knowing, is revealing itself to be the network of the Apocalypse, as we are denied the opportunity to digest all the radical facts around us.

I started this chronicle, I must confess, with a specific end in sight. I intended to lead you through the historical maze of positivism to reach a premeditated and rather obvious conclusion about the unreasonability of religion, of all religions, inevitably diverted from their original etymological purpose, "*religare*," reconnection. I had planned to condemn the false idea that a god made in our image might be guiding us, as we try to comprehend how a message of love and understanding has resulted in hatred and destruction, again counter to its original intent. Might a dynamic of expansion be taking us to a state of maximum contraction, to the originating state where an all-organized universe would become its undesired opposite, *tohu vavohu*, chaos and confusion?

Along the way, however, I came across a much simpler human truth, much more direct, easier to understand. At this point, I stopped.

We are all, each in his own way, and some more strongly than others, incredibly distanced from our own center of gravity, that internal point of balance that makes human life on Earth possible, a reality that keeps us standing upright and able to walk, and makes our bodies function without our conscious control. By contrast, this reality makes us aware of body and mind, a result that is not due to an exterior entity manipulating us from the outside, as if we were puppets. What makes us ourselves is the evolutionary force of nature, which, in our particular case, is based on the fact that there is a center of gravity, a natural force whose source we ignore, but which, nevertheless, is what defines us.

This, my friends, does not exist outside of ourselves. This is not about what others say is right, desirable, something that we force ourselves to accept in order to "appear" connected, even knowing, deep inside, that it is misguided and illogical, something that is, at this very moment, reaching the limits of uncontrollable absurdity. Everything must be tried in order to change this development.

We do not owe life to a nondescript being who, paradoxically, is mostly described as looking exactly like a man, only bigger, more imposing and ubiquitous, as perhaps we would like to be; worse, more serious, who allows a few people to represent him the way they chose, through the most abject and despicable traits humanity (or the lack of it) may carry. And on behalf of whom, unfortunately, such destruction has been perpetrated.

I'm an atheist. I don't believe in God. But it's no wonder my husband Alan describes God as gravity, and it sounds as if I'm finally starting to understand the deep meaning of this unique conception. The ideal God is not the force of gravity *per se*, but our own center of gravity, to which we need to return urgently. One word at a time.

NOTHING NEW UNDER THE SUN

We were having Thanksgiving dinner at our son's house when a friend made the astonishing statement: "My girlfriend and I never talk about politics."

My mean mind went on to extrapolate, concluding that the couple kept their passionate relationship up and running by avoiding any discussion that could generate a disagreement between the two. But what kind of loving intimacy could this be?

"So, Alan, what do they actually talk about?"

"*Uai*, what do you mean? Have you forgotten already? They must talk about their passion, about the stars, about the color of their future children's eyes." (Alan obviously didn't say "*uai*," as we do in Brazil, which could potentially provoke serious doubts about the veracity of this report.)

Here at home, as you know, our long-lasting love has been fed mainly by discord, by the hot, passionate tone of our frequent fights about (almost) everything, which, incidentally, has been described by relationship experts as the ideal recipe for a durable marriage. Who knows? For us it has worked so far, and for over ten years.

More recently, however, our efficient "love-war strategy" has been put to a serious test, since after a long dispute over who's right in terms of politics — American politics, at least — I have come to agree with Alan on (almost) everything. And I fear what will come next, as a result of this dreadful general agreement.

So while we are waiting to see where this will take us, I can't stop myself from laughing my ass off (Alan encouraged me to write "arse") whenever Obama appears on TV stating that "the biggest enemy we face today is the weather," I mean, "climate change." And in the last few days, this has happened every five minutes, especially during the coverage of the climate summit in Paris. Okay, I know it's not funny at all.

What's worse, in his global crusade for an all-encompassing lack of sense, having even been labeled by opposition analysts as "pathological," the American enlightened leader has amassed a lot of support, including from Angela Merkel, the all-powerful European Union leader. As we all know, not so long ago, by deciding to prove her nation the most charitable of all, through opening its doors to hundreds of thousands of refugees (have you realized that they stopped talking about this subject after the Paris attacks?), Merkel ended up creating a problem she does not know how to solve. I'm not even going to share with you the most recent comments from a friend who is in Belgium right now, fresh news from the "front," negating part of the media frenzy. As she has told me in confidence, a little shocked, there are rumors that the "refugee camps" in Germany have several features in common with the concentration... Enough, Noga, shut up already! We're not here to advance hearsay, are we?

Anyway, world leaders in unison had proudly declared this week in Paris that this climate conference taking place in the City of Lights was the best answer to Isla... oops, shut up again, you cannot call these terrorists by their name today without sounding xenophobic, despite the fact that 99% of the current acts of terror are perpetrated by people who make it obvious, loud and clear, they are acting in the name of... Yes. Him.

You must excuse me, but there's no way I can make myself associate these two issues — climate and terrorism — despite the dedication of some patient friends, who rushed to explain to this intellectually challenged person down here that "climate change" causes poverty, insecurity, need, and, as a consequence, terrorism. (Nothing to do with religious fundamentalism, and the exploitation of ignorance with meaningless promises, of course.)

Faced with such logical and direct demonstration of cause and effect, all I can manage to do is to go on laughing. It must be a nervous reaction, I don't know. So they want us to believe that an alleged climate change, that may or may not occur in about 100 years, is a more serious challenge to mankind than a gang of soulless brutes who can kill us without notice, anytime, anywhere, even today? Based on a theory that, apparently, nobody can prove?

It never hurts to remember that the crucible in which this new type of violence is being alloyed (I say "new" because it's based on faith, not on social revolt or something, like the much-missed IRA, Baader-Meinhof, and the like, which were previously limited to national aspirations) is geographically located in a region that has been desert-like and miserable since the times of Harun Al-Rashid, the true Caliph of Baghdad, with his thousand-year old stories of oases and other mental refreshments. Even before that.

All right. I can already envision hundreds of activists, "who mean good," accusing me of being ill-informed,

illiterate, etc. Especially now, when, unable to prove that
the Earth is really heating up (I'm talking about the tem-
perature, okay?), they decided to change their previous
slogan, "global warming" — a famous electoral argument
created many years ago by Al Gore (the said "Al Bore," by
the way, lost the election, but never gave up his private,
polluting jet) — to "climate change," without specifying exactly what "change" they are talking about. In this way, they
will be able to miraculously transmute their cause at any
given time to a more convenient "global cooling," which,
incidentally, is what Alan has been advocating for years.
According to my well-informed husband, the world is actually approaching a mini ice age, mainly due to low solar
activity during this period, which, by the way, is not due to
careless or criminal human activity, none of that. It is only
a natural cycle, one that has occurred many times during
the life of our beautiful planet.

Now, considering we're into laughing for no reason,
I just remembered a Jewish joke, kind of anti-Semitic, but
I'm allowed, so there it goes. Consider my option to make
the main character Jewish as a goodwill gesture on my part.
Once upon a time, there was this opportunistic Jew, who,
inspired by stories of space exploration, decided to sell a
tourist package to visit the sun.

"But, Moishe," asked the worried prospect, "how's
that possible? Isn't it going to be too hot?"

"What's the problem? We'll go at night."

Right. I won't go into details about the total lack of
meaning behind Obama's latest statements, because, frankly, although I insist in laughing, I'm depressed enough. Our
President's main focus is to *pose* as a great global leader,
mainly through talking. Incidentally, he seems to believe
that simply not calling a horse a horse will stop wild horses

from running us over, a shame for the so-called "civilized" world, which seems to feel obliged to embark upon a "liberal politically correct" ship of fools.

As far as I'm concerned, I prefer to end this chronicle with another joke, and you can put two and two together if you wish:

The body parts gathered to choose who among them should be crowned king, or queen, or whatever (today it's always better to leave the gender vague).

The first to make an opening statement was Brain: "This debate makes no sense at all, as the result is so obvious. From up here, I coordinate everything that happens. I see, I hear, I feel. I interpret and understand, I control our actions and determine our reactions to facts. Therefore, I should be king."

Heart replied immediately: "Drop that shit, it's too ridiculous. Even if Brain is declared dead I can go on beating, so it is I who deserve to be crowned king. Now, if I decide to stop, there's no life left to pump. How about that?"

And so the meeting went on, with each party defending its platform, some with more energy than others, until you could barely hear, coming from the bottom, a little tiny voice: "You can stop all this empty talk right this second! There is no doubt that I should be made the king of the body!"

Protest came in unison. What power could that small, insignificant body part have? It was often dirty, stinky, acting imposingly and uncontrolled. Its mere name was considered bad taste among educated folks.

"Okay, then. I'll shut myself down for a few days, and after that we can decide. Agreed?"

And so it was done. After a couple of weeks, the body reunited and Arse was unanimously declared king.

I don't need to remind you that, in the privacy of our unconfessed brilliant thoughts, we probably prefer to see this whole wave of violence, whose name we cannot utter, as an annoying threat emerging from the world's asshole, oops, sorry.

**

P.S.: The pain never stops, seriously. And so it happened that this chronicle suffered a setback and was almost discarded, like one of its predecessors no more than two weeks ago. I'll take a risk and affirm that, as in too many of the action movies we've seen lately (don't give them ideas), the killer couple from San Bernardino was actually "activated" by their "command." What a depressing world, indeed.

THE REAL TRUMP

I was very relaxed, watching TV while running on the treadmill, when the final dialogue in a 2006 *Supernatural* episode (don't judge me too harshly, please) caught my attention.

"Who the hell are you?" asked the iconic good guy, in a plaid shirt. "You're a demon!" he suddenly realizes, utterly surprised.

"Don't be such a racist," answered the blonde, exhibiting her real, weird, black eyes that cover the whole cornea, otherwise looking quite angelic. "Not all demons are equal!"

And cut.

***

On Monday night, I was again watching TV, this time live: Donald Trump's rally in a crowded room, mostly packed with young people who gathered not far from here, in Mount Pleasant, a suburban town near Charleston, South Carolina.

I could hardly believe what was happening. To every

bombastic statement of Trump — who, by the way, is becoming more radical and unhinged by the minute — the mob reacted in an uproar, making the "*hola*" we always see in football stadiums. When a tiny female voice came from the back, trying to utter a protest, it was virtually crushed by the noisy horde — U-S-A! U-S-A! — and greeted by an immediate comment by Trump, perhaps with second, and even third intentions: "I *gotta* tell you, so far the security is not doing a great job, I tell you that."

That was the night after Obama's appeasing, unsatisfying speech about the San Bernardino attacks, when Trump made the "historic" declaration that pushed him down to the "nation's limbo" (did it really?), as he recommended a "ban" of all Muslims and a temporary entry suspension into the country for all practitioners of that religion (the word "temporary" was obviously eliminated from most of the comments that followed). What followed, as Americans say, was that "all hell broke loose."

A couple of days later, I suddenly reached a complete understanding of what's going on in this country right now, an understanding that was inevitably challenged by hours and hours of live commentary from all sources, violently criticizing the suggestions of the would-be presidential candidate. According to Fox News, last Tuesday alone "The Donald" got more than 8 hours of priceless live TV, but if this marathon's outcome will reflect a rise or a drop in the polls, remains to be seen.

The truth is that, when Trump says these kind of things, he is, for better or worse, reflecting the thoughts of a majority of Americans, who in public, however, prefer to act according to the weary canons of political correctness. I even agree with some of his points, I must confess. Mainly because I don't give a damn about this "public code of conduct," which may at times reach a level of total absurdity when practiced by "the left."

Nevertheless, my understanding did not include any of that, but rather that Trump is playing a necessary counter-propaganda role, in the face of the propagation ability demonstrated by terrorist groups. What do you mean, we "leave to them" the primacy of persuasion, and indoctrination?

Trump doesn't speak for "people like us," who are not influenced by slogans, or by what we see on TV (I'm not even mentioning that tonight Alan and I are planning to have dinner in a certain restaurant, in celebration of our 10th "formal" anniversary, just because of their excellent ad on TV). Acting very "patriotically," if I can say so, Mr. Donald J. speaks to the same desperate, ready-to-be-radicalized people, only this time on "our side" of the ideological dispute. And they are very well armed, by the way. Trump is a counter-terrorist par excellence, using the same rhetoric tools that the thugs may use, perhaps fomenting similar dangers. On the other hand, he may be indeed sending a message, not the wrong message, as emphasized this week by so many commentators, but an accurate one: "Don't mess with us, because you will be smashed."

All this is amplified to the nth degree through networked propagation, spread on the Internet and across social media. It remains to be seen if any of these suggestions will be carried out. It will probably never happen, because at the last minute we are hoping a legitimate savior of the homeland will make himself known — a savior of the Republican Party, at least.

Considering all the above, and despite all radicalism, I'm still not willing to support the Democrats, who have already caused us enough harm, at least regarding this terrorism issue. Who will deny that since Obama took office, "radicalization" has reached levels yet unseen? Take the word "radicalization," in its verb form "radicalized," which, as a foreigner, I haven't seen it before. But I could be wrong, of course.

As far as I'm concerned, it is quite clear that the resources put in place to examine new immigrants' "resumes" have serious flaws, or the "Radical Mom" from San Bernardino would have never been accepted, let alone received a resident visa.

Another useful contribution to the "common good" offered by Donald Trump is his courage to say in public, with no censorship, whatever he thinks, whatever a lot of people think, without being intimidated by the media. And I'm not talking about our media or anything like that, but about the jihadists' media, that has imposed so much pain upon us recently. Obama himself seems to believe in their power, as do other co-opted individuals (no, I'm not implying anything here, please count me out).

Not that I want to see blood, but one of these false beliefs is that crap about how boots on the ground will surely be defeated by the Caliphate forces, according to some stupid medieval prediction uttered under the shadow of the old Ottoman Empire, which was actually invincible at its time and terrifying as well. I'm talking about the 13th century, folks! Despite their impressive technological skills, these jihadists still seem to be stuck back then!

Now, let's see who is "more macho," despite the fact that now U.S. armed forces accept women in all positions. I've even heard somewhere that Putin is preparing to fire a nuclear weapon on the bastards' domains. Ouch. I surely hope he won't go that far.

What is fairly certain is that Muslim communities

worldwide now have a serious problem to deal with, and sooner or later they'll have to face it: the growing radicalization that facts, unfortunately, don't fail to prove. Or will someone risk to deny that in recent attacks all the criminals' names denoted a Muslim ancestry?

How are we supposed to react? With hugs and kisses in the middle of a crowd, as they did in Paris? Turning the other cheek? How can anyone be convinced that these are not crimes with some religious motivation, all of that being no more than unjustified prejudice?

Tough stuff. But it is their problem, not ours.

At any rate, there I was once again, running on the treadmill, when I came across another seminal phrase, this time in an old episode of *Law & Order*. So here it goes, paraphrasing Mariska Hargitay, the TV series' Olivia (her original phrase referred to love): "This is not faith; this is brainwashing."

In fact, the FBI has told us recently that when they met online, back in 2013, instead of talking about sex or love like other passionate lovers, the demonic San Bernardino couple spoke of martyrdom, jihad, and terrorist attacks.

What a horror. Therein lies the real danger.

One of Those Years

For M.

Amazing, we're back at that time of the year when, if we allow it, we get carried away into remembrance. It's a little early, I gather, but for reasons I guarantee you will understand by the end of this chronicle, I will be taking a short break starting next week, this time for real, not the usual break limited to the editor's routine in order to focus on the translator's, or the designer's routine, or another of all the roles I may fulfill on a daily basis, if you know what I mean.

I will stop to preserve my sanity. And, if I can, to follow my own recommendation to get away from the social networks for a few days, to+ be able to reflect on the countless events and their consequences we encounter in our daily, hyper-connected rush, *ufa*.

All I have to say about this year that is ending, my friends, could be summed up in one sentence, short and sweet: "I have changed."

I'll go further, though, quoting some things that have left their mark, though not all of them, for if I did that, this would not be a chronicle, but a saga; comprised of, as a friend wrote on Facebook, "one blow after another."

It's amazing to realize that the acts of terror that killed the cartoonists at Charlie Hebdo happened earlier this year; while I'm writing, I still doubt it, albeit knowing it as a fact. This was a year that, frankly, began badly and is ending worse — in terms of terrorism, at least, considering the other attacks in Paris and California.

In 2015, Islamic terrorism — dotting the I's and crossing the t's (great, I expected the original Portuguese expression here to be untranslatable) — shot, with no honor, to the top of our list of greatest fears. For those who live in the U.S., like I do, there was no issue of greater importance, especially if we add to the picture "minor" side effects, such as the immigration and refugee crises, which have taken over the election debate. Therefore, this subject deserves a couple of paragraphs in this convoluted flashback.

This year brought a number of achievements on the personal side, as I became a new immigrant and a Green Card holder — a ten-year Green Card, fortunately, which is very different from the temporary one disastrously granted to the "Radical Mom" from San Bernardino. In all honesty, despite having nothing to hide, I was much more afraid of being "rejected," or even "repatriated," than the soulless jihadist, let's face it. At any rate, I walked a path of opinion from left to right that would have previously been unthinkable, but it came to pass anyway, due to my daily American experience. Or perhaps, as an instinct to survive in a foreign country, I mean, for the love of my Republican husband of ten years, as of December 10 (numerologists, speak now, or forever hold your peace!).

Because of this, I began to see things from another

point-of-view, and to feel more comfortable with the conservative way. I have opted, therefore, to root for Republicans in the upcoming elections, without having managed to choose this or that candidate yet, because, between you and me, it seems the political class has gone awry in the whole world, not just in Brazil. In this week's debate, for example, Jeb Bush, my initial favorite months ago, stumbled so hard over his own words and ideas that I thought he was going to give up his candidacy right there on the debate podium, out of sheer embarrassment for his own ineptitude.

As for the current favorite, Donald Trump, I still cannot see him as President of the United States, but I recognize his important role in bringing up a few issues that have been choking us for a long time, lumped in our throats by the dictatorship of the "PC" — not "personal computer" as it might seem, but "politically correct," a new acronym I have just learned. Anyway, funny hair aside — something the candidate, in fact, makes a point of leaving untouched —, comparing DJT to Hitler is a tremendously offensive trap in which several dear liberal commentators have fallen. And I don't mean offensive to the candidate, who doesn't give a damn, or to his supporters, who are still opting for him no matter what, as shown by his rise in the polls, but offensive to the American psyche.

How could the generous, merciful American people, advocators of common good to say the least, be considering electing a Nazi? It is a scandal, and an injustice of sorts. Not to mention that I can't find a single point of contact between the United States of today and the Germany of the Weimar Republic that preceded the rise (and the subsequent fall, thankfully) of the Third Reich.

These people cannot be serious. Firstly, although

ten out of ten candidates and commentators refer to the economy as "disastrous," I, as a Brazilian, think it's frankly auspicious, let's face it. And the Fed is there to confirm it. I don't see anyone standing in line to receive ration coupons, nor is anyone pushing a wheelbarrow full of dollars eroded by inflation in order to buy one loaf of bread. The Muslims at the center of the discussion — I'm not risking a commentary on whether this is justifiable or not —, are not being "discriminated" against based on their ancestry or religion, but because of a real fear we all have from some members of their community — extremists who kill lots of people without hesitation. Muslim Americans have not had their goods confiscated, nor are they being treated like animals or at risk of being killed and then incinerated simply due to their faith or ethnicity. This, my friends, would never happen in the United States, which proudly affirms its fidelity to the Constitution, whatever it takes.

Okay. I'm going to stop here. One of my potential New Year's resolutions might be to get less upset about what I hear or read, and to keep my distance from the extreme political polarization that has taken over, no matter where we are in the world. Moreover, I promise to do my best in order to put aside my low self-esteem, which poisons this chronicler due to regular doubts and inconclusive thoughts I let out in my work. I wish I had the self-assurance some colleagues exhibit when taking as certainties stuff they have only heard, without any real knowledge of the facts. Worse still, they don't even position themselves as "chroniclers" like I do — a relaxed and confessedly biased genre of writers who are ironic, exaggerated, always highlighting their own personal views about everything, not at all. These other writers pose as owners of the one and only truth.

As for the beloved Brazil I left behind... How sad! Amidst the discouragement and depression that affected us all, due to misfortunes in the economy and politics (thank God fear of terrorism is out of the picture), we are closing the year with the long-awaited news that our credit rating has been downgraded to the "speculative" level. In other words, dear friends, we have lost, thanks to this gang now in office, the costly and well-deserved achievements of the past 20 years, during which we almost put aside our eternal label as a "futureless country," immersed in "third-world-ism." Pure illusion. For our generation, both of citizens and entrepreneurs, this is a condemnation with no hope of redemption: Even if we live up to a biblical 120 years, we will not live to see the country recover. That's right, we have lost a whole lifetime, trying to keep our necks away from the stranglehold, safe from the persistent failure of our initiatives. Enough.

And speaking of failure, depression, and terror altogether, I need to finish this retrospective with a tribute, a deeply sad account that unfortunately set the final tone in this dreary journey. One of our closest collaborators, a dedicated, competent professional, a crucial person for our operations in Brazil, now that we live so far away, took his life last week. Unbelievable... The morning of the exact day on which the tragedy took place, we even exchanged emails! How is that possible? How could a man, who works all day solving problems and helping his customers, go home that night and kill himself, leaving behind a wife and child?

Despite all my talking about bipolar disorder and a chronic lack of happiness, always in the mocking tone of chroniclers, I must say that, despite all the hardship, the possibility of ending it all never crossed my mind. And even if it had...

"I would never allow it!" Alan stated, speculating that with the recent wave of bad news, such reactions would become common in Brazil, as occurred, for example, during the 1929 crisis.

I responded by saying that Brazilians are not prone to this kind of extreme action, since they tend to focus on the humorous side of the worst situations — an emotionally healthy people, I think.

Alan, who usually keeps quiet on some parts of his personal history, once worked as a therapist with terribly troubled people. He proceeded to tell me, quite touched, that in serious situations like this a mere friendly touch on a person's shoulder can change the course of events, along with some verbalized love and honest interest: "Are you okay?"

Who knows what lies beneath the human mind?

The Tzadik does.

See you in January, folks, and have a good one!

CROCODILE TEARS

What makes us human, Bones, is that we can feel compassion and regret.

Agent Seeley Booth, on a *Bones* episode.

Right. This is the first chronicle of the year, and I'm already abandoning my best New Year's resolutions. They didn't last. What can I do?

During the holidays — in which, incidentally, I managed to lie in bed and just watch a bunch of movies, unable to read anything due to my advanced state of fatigue — I considered several interesting topics to address in the future in view of my firm intention to avoid, at all costs, the political discussion that has been poisoning my daily life as a writer.

Alright. This world is definitely not for beginners, and I've been trying to fit in the best I can.

Due to the recent translation activities that I'm planning to prioritize more and more, thanks in part to my own residential situation and my ongoing reliance on translation in order to survive, this was one of the subjects that I had contemplated. At the turn of the year, as I tried to escape reality's voraciousness, while taking advantage of the fact that much of the mainstream media was resting like me, I resumed the old habit of reading scientific journals. One of the articles that caught my attention in *New Scientist* explained "how the language in which we were raised forges our personality," or something like that; I confess that I haven't read the full article yet, since my recent subscription will only allow me full access starting next week. But as of now I'm endorsing the idea, because I experience this on a daily basis: Emigration has its (high) costs, as you already know.

Another interesting subject was the issue of the elected translations of our fondest traditions, such as the myth of Adam and Eve. According to an article published on the *Biblical Archaeological Review*, Eve was made of "Adam's penis bone," not from his rib as we previously thought. I asked myself: What the heck was this "penis bone" business, which I have never heard of?

Many male mammals, it seems, have this bone in their anatomy — *baculum* — to keep their "primary tool" standing with minor effort; and when you think about it, it makes perfect sense, metaphorically speaking. After all, this is all about a metaphor of creation, right? First of all, men have no *baculum* to rely on (in my beloved Portuguese, "baculum" also means "staff, support, steadfastness"), so they have to apply their own energy and resources to keep it up, no pun intended. Secondly, while donating his precious bone to Eve, Adam also gave her the power to raise his "morale" whenever necessary, through the conjugal love that is supposed to guarantee the survival of mankind. We'll leave out for now all the other sexual orientations, for which this essential passionate support must come from other similarly boneless creatures, because endorsing their situation could bring down the new paradigm of creation in the blink of an eye.

Back to translation. The serious "bone mistake" could have been generated by a misunderstanding of the original Aramaic, the kind which abounds in our cultural everyday life, as in the case of "Red Sea" instead of "Reed Sea."

It's easy to understand why and how I could have lost myself in the sheer pleasure of such musings, but then came up another equally exciting theme: the convenience of the dilettantism to which I'm so diligently dedicated. After watching a video lecture that Alan had loved and emphatically recommended (the central argument was that deep down, in their essential nature, all things in the universe are nothing more than "light," or "light energy"), I reached the brilliant conclusion that the more we research, the more lost we get. And to avoid falling into this nothingness, there is nothing better than to stay on the surface, trying to know a little bit of everything without going deeper into anything, or rather, into the nothingness in which a deeper knowledge hopelessly transforms our existence.

Yes. Compulsion. (I could have written "confusion," but decided not to.)

At any rate, last night I watched on TV — this contemporary mix of addiction and recreation that encourages us to stick to the couch, instead of indulging in healthier outdoor activities, especially when the weather is too cold or too hot — a 2-hour documentary about Israeli Prime Minister Benjamin Netanyahu, which led me to conclude that political discussion, although mutant and temporary, is crucial to our understanding of this vast, senseless world. This, despite the feeble attempts of some columnists to convince us that politics sucks, and that we'd be far better off focusing our attention on our own individual selves.

The Frontline episode screenplay presented Netanyahu's journey, from his childhood and adolescence in the U.S. to his political "ascension," let's put it that way. Not only to the highest position in the state of Israel, which would *per se* motivate me enough, but to the status of today's "sharpest politician," as I have concluded recently. The documentary also offered a comprehensive perspective on the evolution — all right, some would say "involution," which I quite understand — of the situation in the Middle East.

Oh, dear, how clear it gets that Obama was wrong from the very beginning! And me too! *Mea culpa! Mea maxima culpa!*

In the first week of his first term, despite having been elected with the explicit support of the Jewish community (in which I include myself), the current President of the United States demonstrated his willingness to take "us" to "the other side," moving away from our traditional loyalties, deeply rooted in our Gestalt since the great war that catapulted this country to the top of the global power structure. If we think of it, his inauguration speech made his Muslim ancestry very clear, along with his proclivity to assist this specific community, which *per se* would not constitute a problem...

Oh well. It hurts even more that, despite his unorthodox and revolutionary disposition, Obama failed badly in his intent, and rather than improving the *status quo* in that explosive corner of the world, his support made the situation considerably worse for Muslim countries, *et voilà*, chaos was instated. Worse still, it is escalating in the onset of this new year, with neighbors attacking each other, ruptured diplomatic ties, beheadings and everything else. Quite promising.

Now, I could very well have managed to avoid this thorny issue, at least in the first week of the year, when all predictions and hopes for the future are still undergoing some level of adjustment. But then there came the already iconic Obama press conference in favor of gun control, in which the so-called "most powerful man in the world" was visibly moved, shedding two or three tears in public.

Let's face it, every human in this world has the right to some lack of control when things get bad. Imagine that, on the same day that Obama wept, I had indulged in more than one hour of deep sorrow precipitated by a computer problem (I won't even mention the serious blow to my self-esteem that led me to such convulsive, uncontrollable cry, which Alan criticized harshly as usual, never offering one gesture of solace). I might even admit that my confidence in Obama's "high sensitivity" was the main reason why I rooted for him in 2008, fiercely defying my husband's strict recommendation and imposing opinion. Which, by the way, ended up proving to be right in, say, 78% of the occasions, the disastrous election of Barack Obama being one of them.

Between you and me, to see Obama cry in public that way — for a well-justified reason, okay, but deep down at the bottom due to his own incompetence in most governmental matters — is like seeing one's father fall to pieces in the most difficult moment, when his strength and support, even if they are fake, were badly needed.

That's no good. Come on. The character at hand is not a "dear sensitive boy," but the Almighty President of the United States.

Other political commentators, far more to the right

than I currently am, did what they could to treat the president's pain with kindness. "I have no doubt of the seriousness of his emotions," one of them said. And then he added: "Although his focus is completely wrong." As for me, I apologize, but I'm not going to lend him my shoulder, offering comfort to this poor, miserable, most powerful politician in the world. No way.

If it is any consolation, you can always account my traumatic upbringing for this lack of compassion and solidarity that I shamelessly exhibit, which is what Alan always does. Or perhaps it was the early loss of my father that turned me into this cold, hateful, manipulative creature, opposed on principle to any conciliatory proposition. So be it.

What I could never do is to start all of a sudden to lie in public, or to my limited audience, for the sole purpose of pretending to be the good guy. On the eve of my 64th birthday, I feel I'm too old for this kind of stuff, sorry, folks. Though the heavens may fall, I'm not willing to concede my cherished honesty and commitment to the truth of my own opinion, whatever it may be. As did Obama, who in his thought-provoking electoral campaign promised total transparency of purpose and actions, one of the first moral pillars that our president unfortunately gave up.

Sad.

Paper Globe

When the handsome, charismatic character entered the Chamber, the world stopped to watch him. With his wide, captivating smile, teeth very white, kisses and handshakes, an irresistible vibration emanated from the nation's highest dignitary — the highest dignitary of all nations in his own eyes.

Soon the reverential silence was broken by a whirlwind of applause, an enthusiastic standing ovation.

"Thank you! Thank you very much! Please have a seat!"

The show was about to begin. Sitting in the audience, captured by the camera time and again, some of the candidates running for the next superstar position watched attentively, trying to memorize the secret behavior code behind the most perfect incarnation, the unforgettable icon of our most idealistic inclinations. What a pleasure! What a thrill!

What followed was one of the most exciting speeches in the whole political season. Standing on the podium, with steady gestures and sparkling, watery eyes, the leading actor carefully delivered his wise words in the perfect tone

— sometimes smooth, other times a little sharper, always effective.

One by one, his countless achievements were listed. And, as expected, a *mea culpa* allowed us to identify ourselves with the inevitable prospect of some setback, of possible failure: "To err is human." And life goes on.

To raise the mood, an uplifting goal was offered:

"Let's make America the country that cures cancer once and for all."

Oba. He nailed it!

His final testimony left nothing to be desired, if we consider a country that has been lacking not only its former confidence in its own institutions, but also in its institutional leaders: "The United States of America is the most powerful nation on Earth. Period. The State of our Union is strong."

Oba.

The problem is, my friends, this is all theater. And I'm not alone in this understanding; even my beloved, ex-unconditionally-admired liberal columnists are pointing it out. Moreover, such falsehood could be detected throughout the patriotic discourse in the bored expression of disbelief consistently displayed by the Speaker of the House, Paul Ryan. The strong, booming country that Obama described simply doesn't exist. According to the Gallup polls, 79% of Americans are "dissatisfied with the way things are going in the United States," and President Obama's "playing to the crowd" will not change this.

Sensibly, Obama chose not to emphasize his *war* on gun ownership in his last State of the Union appearance, while carefully avoiding other equally thorny subjects. But the eager audience was not spared from an apocalyptic remark or two:

"2014 was the warmest year on record… until 2015 turned out even hotter."

I must apologize, but as one of those "pretty lonely" people out there who still want to "dispute the science around climate change," as Obama pointed out — the "ignorant and stupid" part he left unsaid — I'm going to need a sidebar here.

I've been upset by this issue ever since the December temperatures here in our neck of the woods turned out to be hotter than average. Even if I'm not exactly an authority on what is the "average" in this place where I've lived for a little over than a year, yes, I agree: It was hot. Then I heard the anointed U.N. "climate ambassador," Leonardo DiCaprio, giving a speech in Paris to set the tone of the international talks aimed at "saving humans from themselves," if you know what I mean. It has been warm lately, okay, but the truth was, the year wasn't even over... How was it possible to already classify it with such certainty as "the hottest one"?

Alan had reassured me this was not the case, but, as you know, I don't trust anyone, much less him. So I decided to check it out myself, to search for these "decisive data" DiCaprio seemed so sure of, along with "98% of the scientific community," and so on and so forth. The available data was so dubious and convoluted that I doubted a little that any layperson would understand them. Besides, being a carioca by choice, someone who lived in tropical Rio de Janeiro for most of her life, I shouldn't be so startled by an island of warmth in the midst of (in)clement weather. After all, how many "Indian summers" have I been through? Moreover, during the (second) strongest El Niño on record?

At any rate, there he was, the glorious DiCaprio, made even more glorious this week by his Golden Globe — a "Paper" Globe, as far as I'm concerned. Doesn't it sound suspicious that, instead of naming a prestigious scientist for the role of U.N. ambassador, they would opt for a Hollywood celebrity?

According to the Cambridge Dictionary, an actor is "someone who pretends to be someone else." Or, to be more poetic, as required by the situation, "a pretender / who pretends so completely / that he even pretends it is pain / the pain that he really feels," as beautifully stated by the Portuguese poet Fernando Pessoa.

Come on. Wait a minute.

As I write this chronicle, the much-anticipated "Freeze Warning" sign demanding we "let our faucets drip," the same one that I loathed so much last year, was finally planted in the dry grass outside our apartment. It is 45 degrees, a sunny day, cold as hell. It's going to snow on Sunday. This winter some days will be warmer, others colder than the historical average.

End of the sidebar.

Meanwhile, conservative networks were all excited discussing another celebrity's stimulating role — stimulating trouble, I would say: Sean Penn's interview with "El Chapo," acting as a (bad) journalist in the *Rolling Stone* scandal. Spare me.

Fortunately, the political festival was not yet over. A significant share of the electorate could at least feel elated by the discreet, rational and well-balanced response to the State of the Union delivered by our also discreet Governor Nikki Haley. I was proud.

A descendant of *legal* immigrants, Nikki was the exact image of a focused, reliable official. Alan "broke into his happy dance" pointing at me, *et voilà*, I felt valued. I told him I was sorry that our Governor wasn't politically mature enough to run for President this time, in which case we'd have a reasonable option — the opposite of our present, confining situation.

Let's face it, although a new victory by the Democrats is downright unthinkable, the Republican candidates seem to be in a competition to show who's the most irresponsible.

I'm feeling lost here, my friends. We're even doing the math to see what would happen in case we went back to Brazil, where, with the dollar at four *reals* and the devil at large, we would do quite well, I mean, if...

Never mind. I'm just kidding. Back there in Brazil, when ex-president Lula was no more than a future threat, we used to say that, in case he was elected, "the last person to leave the airport should please turn out the lights." Ah, that's right, this was well before Lula, going as far back as the military dictatorship. At any rate, just replace "Lula" with "Hillary" and we're in deep trouble anyway. As we all know, failure is "slow but sure."

At least one dear friend described herself as shocked by my strong, wavering position against Obama and, by extension, against the Democratic Party. The party that we, as intellectuals, as guides of the herd, have a moral obligation to support, as you all know, oh, well, there's nothing I can do about it. All I can say is that people who live abroad don't know the half of it. Living in this country, we are exposed to an overdose of information, with TV channels of various orientations, hundreds of shows to choose from, according to one's line of thinking, and even the C-Span channels, which are truly unbiased.

I can only regret that, wherever we are, the grass always remains greener on the other side of the fence, with no exception. As for my desolate Brazilian friend, who answered my message with a terse "thank you for your explanation," all I could tell her was I would probably end up supporting "The Donald," which would be the *coup de grâce* to our friendship. And for that I was sorry.

The Asian Factor
(Killing Computers in America)

In my seven years as a digital publisher in Brazil, I developed a kind of "affection" towards a specific brand of computers. The machines were solid, trustworthy, and the support was great. For a mere 10% of the computer price I would be covered for two years: A specialist would come to my office in the midst of the Atlantic Forest whenever I needed. Moreover, although "remote access" was not available at the time, the telephone support was impressive, and the agents were savvy: Customers with a little knowledge of how computers worked, myself included, were effectively directed on how to solve their problems.

Then I moved to the United States, where I've been living for over a year. When the time came and I needed a new computer, my inclination was to remain faithful to the same brand. Moreover, their HD-quality screen resolution, crucial to my line of work, was unique in the market.

I carefully chose the latest model, with state-of-the-art features, but my first attempt was a complete disaster: I opened the box and took the computer out, and excited like a child, I plugged it in, turned it on... and perceived immediately that something was terribly wrong. One-fourth of the screen was flickering, with visually disturbing blue, red and green stripes. The graphic processor was defective. I had to return it.

The desired model was now out of stock. I waited. When it became available, I ordered it again, and this time everything seemed fine. The screen was beautiful, the machine appeared to work perfectly. I proceeded to download all my data from the back-up cloud and to install the necessary apps to start working, until... I got "the blue screen of death," caused by some unknown "conflict." Speaking of which, Windows has recently replaced this frightening, alarming expression with a simpler "something did not work out and we must restart your computer," followed by a sympathetic "sad smiley face." Much better.

The support specialist tried to fix the issue through remote access, but promptly warned me that this probably wouldn't work. He was going to mail me a USB media drive. If the computer crashed again, I should restore it to the "factory image," which I ended up doing.

After more than ten days of work devoted to "tuning up" the computer, I realized I was having problems uploading files to the cloud, a key feature in my daily routine. My Internet connection was fine. I was not having any trouble with the other computers in my network. I ruled out other possible issues, like a firewall setting or something, and then decided to call support. Once again.

I have been warned about the diminishing quality of computers, which could be attributed to the declining quality of the manufacturing in China. We once used to joke that all computers made in China came with a secret "spying chip," we should be extra careful. But it was only a joke. The insistently defective operating system was just a coincidence, I was unlucky, and that was all. Except it wasn't. Complaints on the web were all over the place, but I ignored them.

Back to the support session. Being a foreigner myself, I had a hard time understanding the agent's strong Indian accent over the phone, which was solved by switching to the remote session screen. The representative proceeded, with my permission, to download and install on *my* computer one of those "free," commercial anti-malware solutions that always come up with a thousand issues, in order to convince you to upgrade to some premium version that will *protect you effectively.*

"Are you sure you want to install this commercial software?" I asked. "Does your company really *recommend* this software?" I emphasized, feeling truly uneasy.

"Yes, we use this software all the time, no worries. We will fix your computer."

Bingo. My brand-new computer had 1,000 "threats," and I was doomed.

Except I wasn't. These warnings are usually fake, pointing out stuff that does not affect the computer at all, according to my experience.

The support agent then tried to convince me that I should buy premium support access, which would cost 30% of the computer's sale price. Per year. I refused.

I don't remember exactly what happened next, but I ended up talking to this man's supervisor in my broken English, complaining about the agent's actions. The supervisor apologized deeply, and I was transported into one of those Indian movies that show the harsh routine in call centers where supervisors operate like some kind of modern slave foremen.

I deeply regretted the agent's fate, but there was nothing I could do to help. I had my own urgent problems to deal with.

To make a long story short, this week I had another remote session with the Indian call cen... *oops*, the support center in India. This time, the agent spent more than two hours on my computer — for free. It was now a "matter of honor." He would fix my issue no matter the cost.

Except he didn't. He installed the "special tool" that is provided only to premium maintenance plan holders, ran a bunch of tests, but to no avail.

The next morning, I was so upset that I went back to Google, where, as everybody knows, generous computer "geeks" share their knowledge absolutely free. And I finally found a suggestion to check the date of my wireless driver.

It all took less than a minute. I checked the version, and it was outdated. I downloaded the newer one directly through Windows 10, *et voilà*, my issue was solved.

I've been wondering ever since what kind of company would entrust its customer care to the hands of such an incompetent staff. What would be the reason for that? To save some money? To get rid of American jobs? To commit entrepreneurial suicide?

Okay. Let me be clear, here. I didn't mean to criticize all Indian support centers, just this specific one. Adobe support, for example, is truly great; moreover, Adobe's current CEO is an Indian-American. And Calibre, my digital converter of choice and the most customer-friendly software in the world, was also created by an Indian, a computer genius.

As for China, well, according to the latest reports, Chinese industry is not exactly *thriving*, right? I'd better leave them alone, and time will take care of it all.

All this kept me thinking. Maybe some presidential candidates have a point after all. We have outsourced too much, and now we've been hoisted by our own technological petard.

Bernie Sanders' Kibbutz

A few months ago (around June 2015, I guess), I was approached by my childhood best friend, a Brazilian like me who also lives in the U.S. with her American husband, concerning a fund-raiser for the incipient Democratic presidential candidate, Bernie Sanders.

"Can you imagine?" she sounded very excited. "If he wins the nomination, he could be the first Jewish president of the United States!"

I dismissed her.

"Who is this Bernie Sanders guy?" I asked Alan.

At that time, Hillary Clinton was not only the indisputable front-runner, but also the one and only Democratic candidate. Then Sanders appeared as a disposable option — an old, insignificant postulant to the presidential race from distant Vermont.

This week, as Sanders left the White House after a meeting with President Obama, I was fairly shaken. Against all initial odds, the old man had come far, with his 49% in the polls.

I was reminded of my father, a Zionist idealist who in 1950 left everything behind and emigrated to Israel, days after his marriage to my mother. In one of the wonderful letters he wrote her during their brief courtship, he said: "In Eretz, we won't feel like foreigners anymore. And we will be free from worries about money."

My father, one of the founders of Ein Dorot, a kind of preparatory kibbutz in São Paulo, Brazil, also wrote that "good things in life are difficult to obtain, but we must be strong enough to overcome all obstacles, when we are sure that what we seek is fair, and is what we really want. Which I am."

Life in Afikim, the kibbutz in which I was born, six miles from the Sea of Galilee, was not so easy, and the overcoming of obstacles not so fulfilling. My mother got sick, and my parents decided to return to Brazil, much to my father's dismay, or so I thought for a long time. Much later, my aunt told me that, in fact, my father was deeply disappointed with the political machinations of the kibbutz, an institution that proved at that time to be quite distant from his idealistic dreams.

Back in Brazil, my father made a living as a store owner, a businessman, until he died in a car accident in 1972. He was 44 years old. Although he often talked about it — and in my imagination, I believed that he *thought a lot* about it — he never moved back to Israel.

In 1970, I spent a year volunteering on a kibbutz, early enough in the socialist history of the country to experience the unbounded sharing of assets and the delightful unnecessariness of money on a daily basis. But when I visited Israel again in 1998, the situation was different. On the kibbutz where my cousin lived with her family, people were talking about "owning" a car (heresy!), traveling to Europe, and, horror of horrors, using a *credit card* to buy food at the kibbutz grocery store. I don't know where these things stand today.

My point is, socialism is quite passé, and it has proven not so positive for the progress of human society, which is strongly based on ambition and competition. At least, this is my opinion. And I don't believe socialism would be any good for the United States, a strong capitalist nation based on free enterprise, freedom of initiative, and capital gains, very personal gains.

Now, speaking of other Bernie talking points, I have a thing or two to say.

"First of all," as the candidate likes to say, free college and free everything were widely exercised in Brazil over the last few years. The university that belongs to the state used to be one of the best, but it's pretty much in decline right now, thanks to lack of resources, and also due to the political influence in the choice of professors and chairmen. As for the social practice of giving stuff away for free and "helping the poor," these have resulted in the widest and deepest case of corruption the country has ever seen. Nowadays, every initiative or investment proposal has to "pay a price" to the powers that be; but I'm sure these two factors are not so directly associated as I make them appear to be. I'm just a suspicious, heartless shrew, I know.

"Second of all," concerning Obamacare, I have an even more "intimate" experience. As a new immigrant, I discovered I was forced by law to acquire health insurance under the program, and if I didn't, I would be subjected to a fine. But the best option I could find required that I paid $650 a month, almost the same amount as my rent, something I couldn't afford. Not to mention that I trust my health and don't want to be forced into buying anything… so I decided to "go rogue" and risk the penalty, which is significantly cheaper. Fine! My good health for 2016 I place in the "hands of God," and a year from now, I'll be eligible for Medicare, I hope.

Moreover, I have to admit that I'm deeply turned off by Bernie's accent and his weird articulation of some words; but who am I to criticize this kind of stuff, right? Alan can most assuredly tell you. In a few instances, by the way, Bernie and Alan have so much in common that I have even dubbed them "Big Bernie & Little Bernie": two Jews of the same age, both ex-hippies, etc.

Alan, of course, could never be President of the United States. As we all know, short people are not allowed in the Oval Office.

On the other hand, in times like ours, the idea of having a Jew in the White House is truly attractive. I know, I know, although he was raised like every one of us, not only in the Jewish faith but in Jewish principles and ideas of integrity, Sanders barely mentions his Jewish background, nor does the media emphasize this aspect of his ancestry and family tradition. Which, as we all know, is something that defines you.

It kept me thinking. When running for office, Obama always denied his Muslim roots, but as president, he rarely fails to make it very clear, at least in his diplomatic efforts. Maybe the same thing will be true with Sanders, who knows. It demands a huge effort, in fact, to separate oneself from the culture in which one was raised. Even if this influence may be subtle, it never fails to impose itself when decisions are made.

God knows how badly we Jews need an ally in the White House. Oh well. It does not mean I'm going to jump in and endorse Bernie's candidacy all of a sudden. I'm still traumatized by the way I so strongly rooted for Obama in both elections... Alan managed to convince me that I should feel personally guilty for the current administration's lack of support for the State of Israel... This was, by the way, his winning argument to make me change my mind, and finally cross to "the other side."

At any rate, my primary point for this week's chronicle, before I was carried away by Bernie's visit to the White House, was how confused and deceived I've been by political appearances lately. Only a few days before the Iowa caucuses, everything seems to be the opposite of what I hear and feel, and I'm certainly not ready to make a choice. After all, considering my socialist and idealist upbringing, it was not very likely I would opt to criticize the charming, sensitive, progressive, convincing nature of Obama's rhetorical efforts, not in a million years. And what a good speaker he is, tears and all! However, it is mostly empty speech, and worse, produces meaningless results. The sad state of our present world is the most compelling proof of that, and for the moment, that's what I have to say.

As for you, my dear friend, who gave me the honor of your attention up to this point, perhaps fooled by my tricky title, I'm sorry to say that I'll have to disappoint you. No, I don't have the answer to the biggest enigma, the "most well-kept secret" of this electoral race, I mean, the name of the kibbutz where Bernie Sanders stayed in the mid-1960's, which might "have helped shape his political views." My deepest apologies on that matter!

Forty-Five Days

When I opened my computer on that November morning, a Brazilian federal holiday, I didn't know my life was about to change.

I had posted a simple, terse description of myself on a dating website, not expecting much in return. But on that remarkable November morning, there he was.

It was one of the most difficult times in my life. I was sad and more than lonely, taking care of my sick mother, who was in the first stages of Alzheimer's. Living in Leblon, in the South Zone of Rio de Janeiro, I had made it very clear that I could not go much farther than Copacabana, the nearby neighborhood, since I could not leave her alone for more than a couple of hours.

Alan was American, and lived in Florida.

What followed was an exciting exchange in writing. We could not let ourselves go, and stayed connected most of the time. There was no Skype and no texting available. It took us a while to email a few pictures to actually *see* each other. Alan, I later discovered, did not own a computer, and not even a phone. As far as technology is concerned, he was a kind of "caveman," typing from public libraries and the occasional "cybercafé."

The original dialogue, which contained more than 800 pages and allowed us both to get intimately acquainted — a paradox, I know — resulted in a novel that I published in Portuguese a few years ago.

After 45 days of intense dating, I traveled to Florida to meet him in person. This may sound fairly common today, but back then I knew very few people who could have done it. I was 53 years old when I left my life behind and started a new one with him. Alan and I lived together for six months in the U.S. and then decided to move to Brazil, where he was a foreigner for the next 10 years. Away from his homeland. From his family. From his language, yes, it is hard to explain how the language you speak shapes the person you are to a great extent, as science itself had discovered recently.

The person I am as I write in my native Portuguese is quite different from the person I am when I write in English, and Alan never ceased to remind me of that. Therefore, the English language became the (often unwelcome) third person in our marital bed. Not to mention he never learned a word of Portuguese, except the mandatory "*por favor, muito obrigado, cala a boca e cachaceiro*" — please, thank you very much, shut up and "*cachaça* drinker," *cachaça* being the typical Brazilian liquor made of sugar cane he used to drink every Friday in the farmer's market, with a taste similar to moonshine.

When we first met, I truly believed I could speak English. But although I trusted my writing — after all, I had been able to conquer that brilliant, erudite, unattainable American man — I found myself on the verge of panicking at the mere prospect of having to speak it, and the inevitable phone call was my nightmare for days. At some level, it still is.

On the other hand, the English language has also become my best friend, my counselor, the true sponsor of my unique love affair... and my upcoming literary career. I must confess I would have never been able to express myself sexually, as I actually did, in my native Portuguese.

I was raised in a small, traditional town in central Brazil, surrounded by mountains, by prejudice, controlled by our rigid community standards. Every step we took at that time could result in a threat to our "virgin, virtuous selves," "marriage-valued material." Something today has no meaning at all, I understand. I later moved to the more cosmopolitan Rio de Janeiro, but carried with me my persona from Minas Gerais, as people back there used to say: "You can move out of Minas, but Minas will never move out of you."

And so it was that for some unknown, unexplainable reason, less than 36 hours after Alan and I had engaged in a conversation online, we had sex for the first time. In writing.

"New sensations... I've never tried a cyber orgasm."

Alan was truly surprised.

"How lovely... an adult."

"Do you often have sex on the Internet."

"No. Never. You are the first woman I've ever spoken with on the Internet. But when I'm intimate, whatever the medium I am intimate... I have a capacity for intimacy."

"Intimacy is rare. In fact, I've never been really intimate with anyone."

"I thought it was there for me from the beginning... or it was not? When I read your words they were of poetry... of skin and such... I could feel you. Have you never spoken of poetry, of love, with another?"

Apart from our disposition to always tell the truth, no matter what — except for me, of course, when I decided to "stretch myself a little on Photoshop" — and our communication skills, which could inflame even the hardest of hearts and melt every possible resistance, what amazes me still today is the capacity we have shown to transform that promising bud, that little nucleus of an unknown future, into something big, which keeps growing.

We have come full circle, in a way, and are now back in the U.S. I mean, Alan is. And it's now my turn to be the foreigner in the house. Which is exciting, by the way, but not exactly easy.

How difficult it is today for a couple to stay together?

What is love, actually? What is love, after passion had calmed down, after all possible eroticism has been enjoyed, and we are left with the rest of our lives?

Eight years ago, my book was considered "shocking," for exposing the sexual content of an adult love relationship. Even more so because everything I wrote did actually happen, did actually result in two people deciding to be together. One of my readers complained that "sex was delicate, and intimate. It was the most precious thing a woman could have, and it should be kept a secret."

Sex is not delicate. Sex is a force of nature. Sex is *the* force of nature. But in itself, probably isn't enough to build a commitment for life.

The book we wrote together, Alan and I, was a kind of long-term life planning, if I can describe it this way. Every dream we shared online was in a way put in motion during those early 45 days, and had come true today. Well, most of them, since we are still working on it.

Yes, it was a fantasy. At some level, I agree, it was all fiction, an exciting novel written in real time in literary collaboration. There was even a risk that the characters we described would have very little in common with the people we were in our real lives, a risk we would have to face if we ever wanted to stay together.

So now we have finally touched on my real subject today, which is the "working on it" part, something most of us would prefer to leave aside. I don't know how it happened, how our fierce generational struggle for freedom of choice and expression ended up in a kind of coldness and business-like dealing with the dating aspect of our lives. At least, that's how I see it, or feel it. And I regret it.

What I have learned is that, after we meet someone, that "special one," and make an unconscious decision to be with that person, we start building inside that feeling we can call "love." It is the building, not the meeting, that makes it profound, and that's why love is so much more than a "whole" in which you fall, a chemistry, a rush of endorphins that can easily have you addicted. When the rush wears off, the building takes over. If we so decide.

Life is a succession of endless challenges, and as I write this essay, I'm preparing myself for a big one: I'm about to start translating my novel into English. It shouldn't be hard in principle, since I still keep the original 800 pages that were written in English, after all. I'm even planning to leave some of the original mistakes and typos to add an extra flavor to the text, as I did in the Portuguese version.

At any rate, this time the third person in our bed won't be the English language anymore, but our own not so recent past as online lovers. How will the couple today envision the passion of yesterday? Will we love our Internet selves then, as much as we love each other now? And had loved each other back then?

Alan, I must tell you, is very concerned. All these years, as he could never read the original novel, he has convinced himself that it is all about sex, and nothing else, which could be a bit embarrassing at our age, to say the least.

He has no say on this subject, though. The translating and eventual publishing of this novel in the United States is currently the only dream we have dreamed online that is not yet fulfilled, and I'm ready for it.

"No need to worry," I tell him every day. I have just re-read it, and it feels so strong today as it did when we first wrote it. And felt it. After all, these are 100,000 words that had the potential to change our lives, across 4,000 miles, eleven years ago.

Train Wreck

Honestly, I was trying to envision the absolute state of wreckage (pardon the redundancy) my country now finds itself in as something apart from my daily exile experience... when the whole story turned more personal than I'd have expected: A nice woman I know has found herself pregnant during the panic wave surrounding pregnancies in the mosquito-stricken Brazil of these last few weeks.

We have been discussing this, and Alan advised me, if I ever wanted to write about it, I should do it from a scientific, non-biased point of view, an impossible task.

I'm not a scientist, in the first place. Worse, I'm a faithful practitioner and disseminator of hearsay, which is made even more inconvenient by my habit of exaggeration. At least in Brazil, what I write belongs to the literary genre widely known as "chronicle," also characterized by a very personal point of view.

Not that the media have been acting any differently. Whenever you try to dig deeper into anything that has been published, or is still being highlighted in the news, that's exactly what you find: inexactness.

I shouldn't be surprised. I've lived all my life in a

country that Alan could not help but dub "the land of Ab-salokhes" (sorry, I have no idea of how to spell this name), where, according to an old, politically incorrect Yiddish song, lives a black person *mit* [with] a white *tokhes* [buttocks]. Between you and me, there's nothing offensive about it. It's merely the description of a country where practically all aspects of daily life are fraught with impossibility and lies.

All right. This could very well be Brazil today.

Even more surprisingly, all of a sudden, the highly marginalized Brazilian scientific community (some would say, an oxymoron) is now being accepted as accurate and legitimate by the First World. I mean, by U.S. officials, who, on the verge of I don't know what, immediately offered yet another miraculous intervention, aiming at saving the world from itself. Or, at least, from its widespread dreadful disease.

Don't get me wrong. In the field of infectious diseases, especially the ones transmitted by mosquitoes, Brazilian scientists do have verifiable historical expertise. Like, for example, Carlos Chagas, who not only discovered a dangerous illness back in 1909, but also described it and named it — Chagas disease — although he could not find a cure.

Everything I can personally tell you about the *Aedes Aegypti* mosquito is that I encountered it once, more than 10 years ago. Yes, I had dengue fever, at the time the only disease that was described as transmitted by this particular mosquito. And, man, it felt really bad.

The mosquito was said to be a summer plague, thriving in the still waters that accumulated due to heavy summer rains and in those little plates under plant vases. We were all instructed to keep those plates drained, and at the height of the epidemic, government health agents were allowed to enter people's homes in order to empty them and spray insecticide. Cases of dengue were not heard of during Rio's "winter," which, as everybody knows, lasts only a couple of days.

Now, seriously, over the 30+ years I lived in Rio, there was no talk of dengue in the winter months — June, July, August. Which brings us to the suspicious haste in which Dilma's government indulged itself in issuing a world alert, resulting in thousands, millions of travel plans cancellations affecting the upcoming Olympic Games. Why?

Again, I do not mean to interfere with the most desired safety of pregnant women, God forbid. But I can't stop myself from asking why now, why like this, considering the Zika virus has been afflicting Brazil since the 2014 World Cup, at least. Moreover, as the panic spreads, it sounds as if the whole country is doomed, turned into living hell, sunken under a black swarm of infectious mosquitoes. When in fact the focus is quite limited to a state in the northeast, namely one of the poorest regions in the country, where, speaking of which, most of the suspicious cases of microcephaly were, in fact, discarded as being caused by the Zika virus.

Could this be to any degree associated with all the other problems that have been afflicting Dilma's government? Some kind of devilish distraction, maybe?

Okay. I apologize. Better stick to the facts.

One of the most dreadful results of this wave of bad media is that healthy, most likely uninfected pregnant women are seriously considering abortion, which, in Brazil, is an illegal procedure, with dire consequences if money is too limited to pay for an expensive clinic, albeit clandestine. Not to mention the hundreds of healthy fetuses that could be deprived of their right to life. As we all know, panic gets easily out of control.

And why would I waste my time writing about it? The cat is out of the bag, my friends, and there's no putting it back. But perhaps I could, at least, save a few "little angels," as we call them back home — souls ruthlessly dispatched to the other world with no mercy or chance. What a horror. What a shame.

Only this week, I read in the news, the cases of microcephaly, a rare congenital condition now associated with babies infected by Zika, have risen 49%. Odds are that it is not the cases of the disease that have risen, but, in fact, the communication of its occurrence to the authorities. Before its association with Zika, mothers in general did not see themselves as infected, just unlucky. Moreover, the cases of babies born with microcephaly need to be associated with an infection that had taken place in the mother's womb several months before, 6 months prior to birth. Not to mention that in many cases Zika can pass unnoticed, because of the mildness of its symptoms. Yes, it is confusing. Even more so for ignorant women in poor Northeastern Brazil.

So let's us now resort to a little science; if nothing else, at least to save our speculative asses. One of my Brazilian friends, an experienced doctor who now lives in Canada, describes as a must what she calls "the Pasteur cycle": To know for sure if two maladies are related — for instance, the Zika infection and microcephaly — the following sequence of events is required:

> 1. To collect the supposed causal agent, in this case the Zika virus, from a child with microcephaly;
> 2. To cultivate the virus in a lab; and
> 3. To inoculate the cultivated virus in an animal, in this case an animal embryo, thus provoking the disease, that is, microcephaly.

Was any of that done? I doubt it. The doctor proceeded to tell me the story of how, a few years ago, the causal agent of a serious condition, known as goiter, was associated with Chagas disease. The Trypanosoma was found in all the people with goiter, more or less as it is happening now with Zika; but it was merely a coincidence... The same region that was infected by Chagas disease was also afflicted by a serious lack of iodine, the actual cause of goiter...

Not to mention that there is an absence of microcephaly cases in other regions in the world highly affected by Zika, such as the Polynesian islands. Shallow research can inform us that, although it is only now being given a lot of attention, the Zika virus was actually discovered in Uganda in 1948, leading us to the conclusion that there *must* be a third agent in this case, yet unidentified. Or, the poor Ugandans would now have countless microcephalic adults among its population. Unless, of course, they are all dead, forever unreported.

Zika is a serious disease, demanding all possible efforts in the direction of finding a vaccine as soon as possible. Nevertheless, in the current state of decay and debacle Brazil finds itself, this alert and latest news involving Zika and microcephaly should be treated at least with some degree of incredulity. Until further investigation can be done. Before global panic reaches the highest level, which it already has. Case dismissed.

On a final note, in my beloved Minas Gerais the word "train" is used to describe everything, any fact, especially a previously undescribed thing or fact, as this Zika "train." And what a serious train wreck this is, my goodness. The last drop to finally sink the forlorn land known as Brazil.

Elections and Carnival

In Brazil, it is common knowledge that the year only starts once Carnival is over. Or maybe a little after that. Why not extend the "grace" period until the following Monday, right?

True. Brazilians in general love Carnival, the holiday climate, the Samba in the streets, the drinking, the proverbially liberated love-making. Even those who don't like Carnival so much actually love it, because of the opportunity to escape anything that you hate for a whole week, regardless of the consequences.

So Tuesday night, while watching the victory speeches from New Hampshire primary — let's face it, even the defeated candidates delivered "victory speeches," so to speak — an insight hit me: Americans love election time just as much as Brazilians love Carnival. I couldn't help comparing the jumping crowds in New Hampshire to the exhilarating ones 4,000 miles away.

With very few exceptions, such as the outstanding holiday I had once, when I enjoyed Carnival in Salvador, Bahia, with all its passion and nuance — which, on the spicy side, included the sexual pleasure highly ill-advised this year, due to the Zika threat — I'm not the Carnival type, never was. Especially now, when something deep is morphing inside me.

I was never the type to get carried away by national pride either. And I shouldn't confess this, all right, but maybe it happened that way because I long lived in a country where there is too little to be proud of, and diminishing. Better leave this for later.

Therefore, I was taken by surprise on Sunday night, when, just for the fun of the halftime show — I apologize for being such a bore, but I'm definitely not a big fan of sports, sorry, folks — I was watching the Super Bowl on TV, while in my faraway homeland the best Samba Schools were parading for the annual prize.

It was Super Bowl 50, a landmark. And although as a foreigner I can't understand football at all, I could very well fathom the emotion that hovered over the crowded stadium, the perfectly choreographed performances, culminating in a much more mainstream-than-usual Lady Gaga dressed in red, singing the national anthem — the pride, the devotion overwhelmingly expressed by hands over chests and teary eyes.

Mine included. Yes, that's correct. When I came to my senses, I was standing deeply moved in a corner of the room, on the verge of tears for a land (and a game) that is not yet mine.

How weird was that? What was going on?

Honestly, I have never experienced this "patriotic" feeling, not even close. As a Brazilian writer, I have developed a kind of "defensive" style, rarely understandable abroad, always ironic, looking for the pun and for the detestable traits, in order to avoid possible, probable disappointment. Maybe this approach is a kind of superstition to keep failure at bay, I don't know, not that it could ever work. What I do know is that my fellow Brazilians cultivate a self-mocking style, an internal certainty that, although our country is very cool, it is very doomed as well. In Brazil, everything that can go wrong will certainly go wrong, and if it's doing pretty well at some point, it will surely break down in the near future.

And so it did this time, *voilà*, a time which appears to be worse than ever in the course of my lifetime, and I'm fortunate enough to be out of there.

Nothing is that simple, of course. Every exile knows that nostalgia is part of the game, and to be away does not protect you from the possible shame caused by so many disasters at once.

And yet, at some point your psyche starts to change.

I've always seen myself as a political being, and for a writer, especially for a Brazilian writer, it is far more inspiring to be in the opposition — on the kvetch side, if you know what I mean. Except that the kvetch side has grown too wide, embracing a large percentage of the population — social media being the kvetch media par excellence. But for a political being, for whom politics speaks much louder than any Samba song, the American election season is a veritable feast.

And here I am, taking joy in all these empty speeches, passionate rallies, mobile crowds, even if I cannot truly feel what they feel, get what they get, vote like they do. I'm *infected* to the point of convincing myself that all these hours in front of the television, listening to the endless discussions and the changing opinions of the so-called "pundits," will help me improve my English once and for all. At least, I seem to have learned enough to point out the mistakes they make on the air and laugh out loud:

"Alan, why do these *enlightened* people make so many mistakes in English? What a difficult language, my God! Even the best cannot speak it properly!"

If it's any consolation, I criticize them for fun. And that too shall pass.

Different from well-informed Brazilians, who daily exercise their national — well-justified — contempt, Americans in general are very outspoken when it comes to the love of their country. And let me tell you: This feels really good, and very unique from a foreigner's point-of-view.

Well, maybe I'm really morphing, after all. And guess what: I'm now living in a place where the democratic game appears to be the local Carnival, a most appreciated show. It lasts much more than an extended four-day weekend, almost a whole year, the last in each four-year period. And even if the work never stops here, and the holidays are scarce, it is a lot of fun, indeed. Notwithstanding its very serious consequences.

AMERICAN DIVERSITY

I was climbing up the stairs when I saw her outside her door, always kind, delicate, looking great.

"Are you coming from the gym?" she asked.

My leggings and sneakers, plus my disheveled gray hair pulled back with a black plastic clip, made that obvious, fortunately.

"I am. Do you want to go there?"

She's new in our building, so I figured she wouldn't know where the gym was, and immediately entered the "helpful mode." But she seemed pretty self-assured as she answered in perfect English, perfect at least to my foreign ears:

"No. I'm going to check the mail."

My new neighbor is Chinese. At least she looks Chinese, and the language she speaks on her iPhone sounds Chinese as well.

Our relationship did not have a particularly good start. The Bostonian designer who had lived next door for a couple of months had left a few weeks earlier, a real gentleman. Coincidentally, when I met him for the first time, I was also disheveled, coming back from my daily run —

don't jump to the conclusion that I spend my whole time running, or that I'm always disheveled, though the latter is not very far from the truth. Although we had only exchanged a couple of words on a few occasions, his tall, charming self decided not to leave without a thoughtful gesture, knocking on our door to say goodbye. As I said, a perfect gentleman, and for the purpose of this chronicle I must add that he was black, and handsome, and highly sophisticated. I'm not sure if you remember, but I mentioned him once in a previous chronicle, when I argued that I had not witnessed any trace of racism in this country, at least not anywhere near me, thank God.

Now back to the Chinese woman. I didn't have the faintest idea of who had moved in next door after the designer left, but it didn't look encouraging. My first problem was that the new neighbor left his or her (remember, I still didn't know who the neighbor was) garbage piled up in stinking white bags every morning, before he or she left for work, and there it stayed, rotting the whole day, until my friend, the garbage man, came to collect it at 8 pm. Coming from the gym (once again), I could see the garbage can provided by the "Valet Trash" service sitting untouched, pristine, on the apartment porch.

I complained to the management. To make my point, I photographed the white bag on one of its worst days, overflowing with organic waste, leaning against the wall outside the unit door, and emailed the picture to the manager with an unfriendly note. I honestly felt I was entitled to both, pic and note. After all, although we moved here intending to stay less than six months, while our house was being built, this happened a year and a half ago, making us one of the longest residents around, or so I was led to believe, thanks to the high local rotation rate. I went even further with my unpleasant diatribe, complaining about our outside lamp that had burned out long ago, resulting in total darkness when we arrived home at night: "I've never realized that our bulb had burned out... the previous neighbor always had his light on, which is not the case with this new one, who is not so generous."

The next day, the trash can was outside the apartment, with the white trash bag appropriately inside it. Although I did not manage to teach my neighbor that the can should only be out between 6 and 8 pm, when the trash collector is supposed to come and get it, I was satisfied. Sort of.

Don't get me wrong. This trash-collecting rules were something I had a hard time complying with when we first moved in, especially considering how "*yeke*" I am — a somewhat derogatory Yiddish term for a very strict German Jew, who demands everything to be done by the book (people don't usually qualify themselves that way, they leave it to others). So it was only natural that I judged my new neighbor with the same rigor.

As a matter of fact, I have never been good with neighbors. I'm quite an "isolationist" by nature, and I'm not very friendly by principle, kind of a loner, if you know what I mean. One of our neighbors back in Brazil had advised me that the easiest way to feel at home in the U.S. would be to join as many community groups as I could, especially the ones dedicated to "people my age"... the horror! But despite my best intentions, I have never been able to feel at ease with our *real* neighbors, in our *real* neighborhood, the one where we're truly planning to invest in, up on Paris Mountain. My first encounters with them were cold and distant, to say the least. This included the threat of a lawsuit because of our "setback ambitions."

Only recently, as our lot is finally cleared of the forest — sorry, environmentalists — and ready to build on, I have started to feel warmly welcomed, since anytime we go there to meditate about our future house, a friendly neighbor comes by to tell us how pleased he is to have us nearby. And so are we: What goes around, comes around.

Back to reality, to our dark 600-square-foot apartment, I mean. It was Friday evening, and I was coming from the supermarket carrying a bundle of bags. I must also add that there's no trash collection in the apartment building on Friday and Saturday nights. And before I learned where the communal waste container was, or that there was one, I had to cope with the foul smell inside the house over the entire weekend, a real hassle. But now, as an expert, every Friday evening, after I put away the groceries, I walk outside to throw away the trash, it's already routine.

So that night, as I left our apartment with my humble black bag, I could smell the fumes coming out of the overflowing trash can by the neighbor's door. I did not hesitate for a minute before grabbing the bag and leaving a note taped on the door:

> Hi,
>
> Your trash was full, and quite smelly, by the way. So I took it to the waste bin for you. It was quite heavy!
> Maybe you didn't know that there is no trash collection on Fridays and Saturdays, so either you keep it inside, or you take it to the waste bin yourself.
> In case you don't know, the nearest bin is by the mailboxes, to the left.
>
> Best,
> Your neighbor

No more than five minutes later, I heard a soft knock at the door. I opened it up in my running outfit and… disheveled, for a change, since I had gone shopping straight from the gym and had had no time to change. There stood a young Chinese man in a dark-blue polo shirt with a company logo, smiling warmly, with my note in his hand:

"I hope you did not mind that I took your trash," I said, apologetically.

"Not at all, I'm the one to apologize… I don't know why they did not get our trash last night."

"Ah, yes… maybe it's because the trash man is really sensitive," I said. "He usually does not touch the trash if the can is overflowing." I spoke like the class-A trash specialist I had become.

With half of her body stuck out of their door, I could see his wife, an elegant woman I had only heard until that moment, as she spoke Chinese on the phone all the time. She was barefoot (as is the custom in China, when you're inside the house), so I could see that she was very short. She was actually gorgeous, very well-dressed — all in black, lace tights and all — putting my everyday lack of elegance to shame.

Our neighbors were a nice, young Chinese couple, whose English, incidentally, was way better than mine. I felt immediately friendly towards them, understanding that where they came from there might not exist a "Valet Trash" service. They both work all day, drive two huge American cars, and are often gone for the weekends. Yes, I started to pay attention.

My whole point here is how great American diversity really is, how inspiring it is that people from different backgrounds are able to live together, enjoying the civilized qualities of a first-world nation. In the case of foreigners, provided they are legal immigrants, residents, or visitors with work permits, of course.

Why not? After all, I invested quite a lot to get my permanent residency, and I'm on my way to citizenship, which will finally allow me to vote and influence the quality of life in the country of my choice. Which is quite different, by the way, from the place where I come from: It feels truly positive that this is a law-abiding country, where the rules have value and are supposed to be respected. And I hope it will remain this way for years to come.

THE MAJORITY REVOLUTION

"**N**u, Alan, tell me, do you think these guys were the good guys?"

We had just finished watching *Trumbo*, the historical drama about Hollywood writers and the McCarthy era.

"Who?"

"Dalton Trumbo and his crew."

As we all know — well, maybe not all — during the Cold War, in the late 1950s, the best screenwriters were blacklisted as communists.

And they were, indeed. Communists, I mean.

Being a Marxist at that time was practically mandatory if you were an artist, an intellectual, a person with higher values and an elevated sense of justice. It was also a crime of treason in the United States, a "threat" to homeland security.

During those "happy times," the world was practically black and white. There was no space for doubt or debate: Although they were persecuted, accused of criminal involvement with a forbidden ideology, it was perfectly clear to everyone with a reasonable IQ and level of erudition who the good guys were, which relegated to the government the role of keeping people apart from the finest artistic creations, a kind of "prohibition of ideas." For their own "good," for their own "protection." Fascists.

Today, in my opinion, we are not so lucky. For every issue, there is a myriad of interpretations, for every idea a thousand memes in quick propagation. Moreover, we feel deceived most of the time (I know I do), led to believe that everything is the opposite of what it appears to be.

Take the progressives, for example, usually associated with the Democratic Party and traditional higher ideals, such as freedom, equality for all, health care, help for the poor, etc. The speech is still the same this electoral season, although dislocated to the far left represented by Bernie Sanders, whose public ideas, let's face it, would have been more than enough to justify his living under a smoke screen back in the 1950s. It is no wonder the 74-year-old is carrying today's youth along on a wave of unprecedented idealism, by his hopeful promises of free this and free that, including tuition and health care. And let's not forget, all this spread a million times through 24/7 sharing on social media.

Has the world changed, or have we? Yes, we were also that way, not so long ago. (By "we," I mean Bernie's contemporaries, like Alan and me, well, more or less, as I'm only 64). Now we have lived a lot. We must know better.

The problem is the progressive agenda, eager to guarantee that all citizens were treated equally, not by the force of reason, but by the force of law, has locked the so-called "majority" into a room in the back where all freedom of expression is under constant watch. Instead of banning some prejudiced ideas, it banned instead the words that represented them — a "prohibition of the lexicon." Take for instance the "N" word, the "G" word, the "F" word — which, by the way, a few years ago nobody reasonably educated would ever say in public. The result is, in my opinion, that everybody is befuddled, intoxicated with information, not knowing what they can or cannot say. Or think. Or do.

Who are the fascists now?

People today suffer from a complete lack of historical perspective. This week, for example, poor John Kasich of Ohio was massacred because he said in an interview that he had been helped in his state senate campaign, many years ago, by "women who left their kitchens to support him." Hillary, of all people, jumped down his throat immediately — let's face it, Hillary is the instantaneous poster girl for any cause that might boost her campaign, no matter where it comes from, or what it implies.

But, people, come on: Kasich was talking about something that happened in 1978! This is ridiculous! I wish I could tell you what percentage of women had full-time jobs at that time, but I found no data. They were stay-at-home moms for the most part, yes, they were, and not ashamed of it. It was just how things were.

Don't get me wrong. As far as I'm concerned, all I ever wanted was to have a career, to be out in the world like anybody else. Still, I was raised by my mother to get married and have children, nothing else. The concept of double shift most of us now take for granted, or as a normal obligation, was utterly unknown back then, and I grew up through this ingrained conflict.

I believe this to be one of the reasons why I feel so detached from people in their forties with whom I work closely today: They were born in the mid-1970s, on the other side of the complete reversal of social expectations that had taken place over the two previous decades, which people my age have witnessed (and suffered) all through our childhood and adolescence.

More or less like it's happening today, for those who were born in the 21ˢᵗ century.

On the other hand, I feel constrained, suffocated by the political correctness of our days, the need to respect a kind of widespread diversity that we didn't know while growing up in a world that was, as I said, mostly black and white. With only one model of telephone and only one phone in the house — if we were lucky, with a coiled cord long enough to carry it into our bedrooms, in order to get some privacy. Teenagers being urged by their parents to "get off the phone" and free the (land) line were the norm as well.

There might be a lot of people like me out there, among the not-so-silent majority holding signs while following the Trump phenomenon, hair and all (the hair issue being quite forgotten by now). He might have an answer after all, a solution for our anxious, our somewhat undefined feelings, as we can see an ever-growing gap between what is said and what is done, or what is accomplished in real life. But I have to admit, I was truly frightened by the enthusiastic mob's tone during Trump's speech in Atlanta this week, and also by the candidate's bombastic style, his very effective manipulative skills: "We're gonna win! We're gonna win so much that you will beg me, 'Please, Mr. Trump, let's stop winning, we are tired of winning all the time.'"

So here I am, with no candidate in hand, fearing Donald Trump, and at the same time secretly rooting for him just a little bit — and for that I feel compelled to apologize — just to see if his bluntness and openness, along with the enthusiasm of his followers, can bring some radical, effective change, the change we hoped for in 2008, and that has failed us ever since. And I don't mean a change in the style of the White House, but in our personal, highly watched, and socially censored daily lives. Which, by the way, is the exact opposite of everything we might have dreamed in our own radical revolution, back in the 1960s.

A change for the better, I hope. Better for all.

Okay. At least I did not lose my mind to the point of affirming that "Trump's campaign is going to end with the candidate's assassination," as tweeted the other day by a *New York Times* columnist. He later apologized and deleted his tweet, so I guess everything is all right now. Right?

You surely could ask why don't I support Bernie Sanders. Well, I'm old enough to know what lies behind any alleged sincerity with very scarce chances of coming true: a cold, frustrating, all-encompassing void. It has not worked in the past, and will probably not work today. Not to mention his denial of his background, not a good proof of character, in my opinion. Polish ancestry? Give me a break.

All these reflections, of course, would be only valid in a world that has not lost its mind entirely, mostly due to how easy it is to express an opinion nowadays. Then change it, or just delete it.

The Last Invoice

A couple of years ago, when Alan and I started "dreaming" — I mean, planning — our next move on the chessboard of life, I came across a miraculous way of guaranteeing a secure retirement, called a "reverse mortgage."

Once we reached the other side of the Equator, and the time finally arrived for us to build the necessary house, I decided it was in our best interest to go to the bank and explore our options.

Let me get that straight: I am not so excited about reverse mortgages anymore, and not only because of the money. In fact, my old, apparently relentless enthusiasm has been recently rekindled by a new publishing company in the United States and by a few valuable partnerships that will allow us — me — to move forward, hopefully with some success and increasingly good foreign ties and translated titles. So I'm bidding farewell to retiring any time soon.

At any rate, we still had business to discuss at the bank, so we headed that way in our best clothes, sets of drawings under our arms.

"It's not that we need your money at this point, but,

well, I would like to know what our possibilities are," I said, sounding bold.

"I don't advise you to apply for a loan today," answered the bank manager. "It will cost you, and you don't exactly need it. I advise you to move forward, and if at some point in your project you need our help, we will evaluate your property and discuss an interest-only option."

This sounded okay. I was reassured. Of course, if we were in Brazil… in four or five months, when we would supposedly need some support, the bank manager would probably be gone, replaced by someone else (in Brazil, they make a practice of "rotating" bank managers, to avoid any possible closeness with clients), and the interest rates would have doubled, or tripled, or worse: The available loans would have disappeared from the bank's agenda.

In all honesty, for my own survival purposes, I'm trying my best to sever my ties with Brazil right now — not the emotional ties (for this will never happen, nor do I want that), but the business and financial ties… and expectations. Frankly, it is impossible to go on living with a threat constantly hovering over my head, like I have done for most of my productive life. I'm even ready to renounce my significant retirement funds, which at best would amount to, hmm, let's say, around US$200 a month, and I'm not even qualified yet. I would have to go on working and paying taxes (in Brazil) for another 5 years, at least. Not "gonna" happen.

While I was entertaining these divisive thoughts, my accountant wrote me to say he would soon be dropping our account, since, due to the (eternal) Brazilian crisis, he will no longer be working for small companies like mine, rather focusing on a single client. His call, no doubt. But there's no dispute his decision left me out in the cold. What was I supposed to do, 4,700 miles and a bunch of new economic rules away?

I was already considering communicating my change of residence to the Brazilian equivalent of the IRS, not that this was optional. After 12 months abroad, this report is required by law, but I was hesitant. This would result in serious changes to my company's tax regimen — benefits and such are not available for residents abroad — and the fine for non-reporting is small, to the point of insignificance.

Therefore, my accountant's notification did not fall on deaf ears; on the contrary, it set me in motion. I'm not a procrastinator by nature, much to the contrary. So the next day, I went to the "IRS" website and started to fill out the form.

I have no idea of how it happens, but as you all know, one's emotional state has a huge effect on computer apps and such: I went to the wrong year's page and had to repeat the process a couple of times. After I was finally done, I was left in a state of depression and sad prostration I could hardly explain. Or fight against.

Friends, I was depressed for the whole week. But I had to move on, and I had put a deadline on myself: Starting March 1st, I would not write any invoice from or receive any bill directed to KBR Brazil. As I rushed to communicate to my authors, the company — we maintained our initially proposed transparency to the very end, against all odds and convenience — was about to be encompassed by its younger sister, the much more stable KBR LLC. Despite crying every day, I was quite effective in keeping my head up, negotiating new international distribution deals, all converted to the much more stable American dollar — the Brazilian *real* getting less and less real, at least for me. What can I do?

The awaited and much feared day arrived quickly. It was now time to create the last invoice. I was exhausted — emotionally exhausted, at least. And here a sidebar is necessary.

An "invoice" in Brazil is nothing like you Americans are used to. What do you mean, a simple Word document with your company's name and a randomly assigned number? Not in our over-controlled, over economically chaotic Latin American country, no, siree. As one can fathom from the sorry state of our state-level corruption, a lot of effort is put in place to guarantee everything and everybody complies with the rules, and the invoice-making process is no exception.

First of all, you need a software approved by the government, or at least a subscription with an authorized invoice-issuing company, believe me. You also need a magnetic card that you need to renew every one or two years (meaning, to pay for it over and over again), also provided by a small bunch of officially authorized happy few. Once you fill out the form with all the data and requirements previously approved by the government, it is impossible to cancel it, or even correct it, depending on the data you need to alter. It's even more serious if you consider that, once you click "Send," the invoice is sent directly to the tax office.

And don't you go imagining that once these rules are established, they are conveniently set in stone, so you can relax and proceed. Not at all. The government keeps changing them and adding new ones, which makes every entrepreneur's life impossible without hiring a permanent and highly competent accountant.

Now picture me in another country, not exactly following the latest legal developments in Brazil — let's face it, Brazilian developments are overwhelming and difficult to follow wherever you are — and worse, abandoned by my accountant. End of the sidebar.

On the appointed day, I woke up early, took a deep breath, fetched the orange plastic bag where I store all my Brazilian cards and tokens and stuff like that (the workings of our banks security system will be left out for another text) and prepared myself for the big event.

Bingo. I had filled out the form to register a new client, *et voilà*, for some unknown reason the "system" wouldn't accept the name of the city. I tried a few times, always getting the same error message, and then decided to call Customer Service, which, miraculously, is quite efficient, even from 4,700 miles away. Not that I tell them where I truly am, right?

After a few comings and goings, everything was finally set. The invoice was sent and the last book delivery was on its way. KBR Brazil was about to cease to exist, after 7 years of pioneering and no small struggle. Yes, for those of you who still don't know it, this humble chronicler was the first editor in Brazil to publish an e-book in Portuguese. I was set free, after a long career of being the first this and the first that in Brazil, after being forced to react to all impossibilities that ever crossed my mind and that I managed to overcome, no matter in which field. I was a furniture designer, then a jewelry designer (Alan will certainly complain about this one, for he does not fancy me as a jewelry designer, which he claims he was also once), an art director, then a graphic designer, and finally a writer and editor, when at last I could refer to myself as a professional without any shame. And writer and editor I am, now loose and lost as a floating balloon released by a careless child.

It was a terrible sensation, albeit a much awaited

one. I had finally ceased to be a Brazilian entrepreneur, a position I don't plan to occupy ever again. And it hurt. It still does. But for the first time in my troubled existence, I'm finally willing to let it go, to surrender, to "let the universe help," as so many credulous people recommend. I sincerely hope it does.

As for the team of 200 and something authors in our Brazilian portfolio, and counting, I ask you all not to feel abandoned, suddenly left out in the cold. I will make you a final promise, which I'll do my best to honor in any way I can. Rest assured I'm not abandoning you, leaving you behind. Much to the contrary, I'm carrying you along to a better, more stable future. We are all writers of the world from now on, and better still: paid in American dollars. You may spread the word.

***

Now, on a short note, and on very short notice, I could not publish this chronicle without acknowledging the much-awaited light at the end of the Brazilian politics dark tunnel, as the former working class hero Lula da Silva was taken for interrogation to the Federal Police headquarters. More on these developments next week, I hope.

I Flip-Flop, and So Should You

Let me get this straight: I never liked Hillary Clinton in the first place.

When, back in 2008, I devoted all my energy to help elect President Obama — okay, no more than a bunch of empty words, and worse, in my native Portuguese that nobody reads — I mentioned something like "crocodile tears," concerning her theatrical reaction to women's pain, or to a particular woman's pain: her own.

Today, when I see her flip-flopping to fulfill some empty expectations of her attentive audience, I don't feel compelled to say anything. Although I might have, if I chose to believe what the opposition press consistently says about her.

You might ask, what the heck is the "opposition press"?

Back in 2008, I have to admit, I hated Fox News with all my might, just as it's hated today by the so-called "leftists." I mean, the "opposition" media. Back then, I did not hesitate to bravely face my Republican husband, since everything seemed to make perfect sense: It was me against him and in favor of half of the world.

We won: me and that world half. There was no doubt in my mind that I was right, and my husband was wrong. Which, as you know, is a steady basis to keep any marriage going: the wife being right and the husband wrong. This exalts our "women's rights" and puts things in their correct perspective, granting the man in the house his famous last words: "Yes, darling."

Life moved on. We're now living in the United States, where, in this electoral season, I feel more and more out of place.

I feel displaced in the first place, well, because I am. More importantly, I feel terribly displaced, because, since setting my feet in this wonderful country, I have started to see things quite differently, transforming myself into a stranger in my own eyes.

Therefore, I don't support Democrats anymore. I don't hate Fox News anymore. I don't loathe my Republican husband anymore, neither do I challenge him, when politics is the topic at hand. And this is not only because right now, more than ever, my survival depends on his.

"I worry about you," I said, after his n^{th} bout of coughing.

"No, you don't. You worry about yourself. What would you do if I was suddenly gone?"

Well, he's right. Sort of.

My dependency on him has grown exponentially, not only because I'm now a foreigner in my own home, but because more and more, I can't see myself in this world without him, and I'm getting too old to pursue a new love, oh, well. On the bright side, some would call this "true love."

Maybe I should buy a new car, one I could drive more easily than that old Mercedes we bought a year ago, I told myself last night, with all the depressed pessimism a sleepless night can bring. At any rate, this would not help the fact that I would need to pump gas on my own, something that mostly happens in the United States, if you did not know.

I could lump all these things together in the same pot with my latest financial insecurities, but none of them would explain why I have changed my mind about politics so completely, now that I'm living on American soil.

And then there is Donald Trump.

I started to pay attention to the man because my husband happened to like him at some point. And no, my husband is not part of the #middleagedwhitemalematters crew with their hateful rumblings, mainly because he's not middle-aged anymore. He is just plain old. I could say, "old and wise," exactly the type that convinces you, in the wink of an eye, that he's "always right," and that would do him some justice. So it was curious to see that, when "his" presidential candidate was viciously attacked by his "own party," he started to... flip-flop. Oh my.

Between you and me, if we were to flip at this point, who would we flop to? Ted Cruz?

"*Cruz credo*," I would say, in my native Portuguese that nobody reads. Which would loosely translate into "God forbid" or "knock on wood." Speaking of which, politics is not some "gift of God" matter, no matter what all these humanly flawed candidates dare to say.

As I said before, I supported Obama with everything I had, and this got "us" into a situation where "our" President *looks* very good, very presidential indeed, but the world out there is far more dangerous than it was when he took office, not to mention "all that mess." I'm just observing. What else can I do?

I can surely pay more attention this time — go less for the guts and more for the brains, or is it the exact opposite? That is, if reason counts, which apparently it doesn't. Go more for earthly matters and less for the dream, if I dare to dream at all, now that my short-spanned future is here in the U.S. At least while I have a spouse, with whom I don't want to fight.

Now, what if the "opposition" press is right? What if the Mussoliniac and Hitlerian theories are right? I could never forgive myself.

Come on. I still read *The New York Times*; but if I were a reasonable person, I would be disputing this habit right now, after their vitriolic editorial against Donald Trump. I was awake into the night when I read the first comments, first coming from Trump's supporters, or at least from people who don't see him under such a diabolic light. And then the Trump haters jumped in, and on *The New York Times* website, they are in exceeding numbers.

As people in this country now read only what feeds their made-up minds, just like anywhere else in the world, I'm restraining myself and choosing to act as an outsider, a mere observer. As much as I can. As far as I can, since at some point, I'll be forced to position myself, which, I admit, I'm still not ready to do.

It does not stop me from asking myself, why did I decide to change sides? Why now, that I finally succeeded in settling here, in this dreamlike first-world nation... that appears to be going downwards like every other nation in this world? We never cease to witness the ever-growing human stupidity, now far more encouraged than ever before, as we all have unlimited access to spread our own misinformed opinions about everything that matters most. To our own selves.

Long gone are the times when we could turn ourselves to *The New York Times* or the likes of it for some kind of highly informed, intellectual insight. The poison has spread, my friends, and the poisoned ones are us.

On the personal side, if Trump is elected and the world goes to hell in a hand-basket, as predicted by the leftist harpies; or, worse still, if Hillary gets elected and the world goes to hell in a hand-basket, as predicted by the rightist harpies... lucky me, I can always go back "home." Where, to my utmost pleasure and simultaneous pain, ex-president Lula, a world-famous "hero of the left, father of the poor" is about to be indicted for his corruption crimes. Which, by the way, is not an unexpected outcome for leftist and populist policies. This time, the result is a broken country, devoid of all possible hope in the short run; so who is the devil now, and where does he abide?

Time will tell. If, of course, we manage to survive our self-made hell.

It could do us some good to be reminded that, despite the fact that Trump might have struck a nerve, Mussolini and Hitler thrived in countries that were ravaged by poverty, hunger and humiliation, which is not remotely the case in the United States today.

In the end, my insomniac self-advice might have been right: I should have skipped my chronicle today. Or maybe, out of hopeless desperation, I may have made a few relevant points, hopefully worthy of some consideration, after all. The least we can do is say what's truly on our minds, day after day, before it gets corrupted by other people's panic.

When reality is in such a state of constant shaking and change, flip-flopping feels like the right way to go, much like the ever-movable truth. At least until the final presidential vote, which lies months ahead.

Meanwhile, I'll flip-flop. And so should you.

Brazilian Brouhaha

"**I**'m enjoying this whole brouhaha in Brasilia so much," a friend posted on Facebook on Tuesday morning.

I wasn't.

I was panicking.

I have been progressively severing my ties with Brazil over the last few weeks, but not without paying a psychological price. As I wrote before, I had decided to close KBR's operations there and transfer all my business activities to the U.S. This was my last month of a double life. I was planning to close my Brazilian bank accounts by the end of the month.

As you might recall, our move to the U.S. was predicated upon the fact that, after a whole year of trying, we managed to sell our house in Serenity Valley. Next, we struggled to transfer our assets — legally, of course, with the exchange currency moving up and down on a crazy swing — to a bank in Greenville, where we were planning to build a new home. We still are.

Many years ago, when I still saw myself as a person of "faith," an astrologer friend told me I had some kind of "heavenly protection" that stopped me from hurting myself, or overextending myself in my business adventures. I don't remember the dream *du jour* at that point, maybe a recipe book or a vegetarian restaurant, since for a while I fancied my cooking skills. So, basically, I was safe. And, in all honesty, I don't know what took hold of me on that dreadful Tuesday.

Maybe, as mentioned earlier today by another friend who had also moved to the U.S. a few years back, my fear was triggered by an old "panic gene" inherited from ancestors who had to escape the pogroms in Eastern Europe. Although I can't remember any family stories of that sort, despite the fact that my father's family did travel from Poland to Brazil in 1929. Being a Jew, you actually never know.

My memory actually does not fare so far back in my personal history, so I don't remember consciously, but there might be some kind of painful remembrance of the Military Coup in Brazil in 1964, delicately dubbed "the '64 revolution." I was 12 years old, and after a short period of tanks in the streets, everything went back to normal, or so I thought. Only this morning, I could imagine the kind of fear my parents must have felt at the time, both in their early thirties, with two young children to raise and support.

My teenage years went by through the "years of lead," but as I grew up with some kind of protective aloofness, I had a pretty normal life. Eventually, the pressures of the dictatorship abated, and we were back to democracy, albeit with frequent and radical economic crises.

I don't want to recall all the hardship I had to overcome, being a Brazilian entrepreneur and "slightly artistic" my whole life. It has passed. It doesn't matter.

At any rate, when I woke up Tuesday morning with an excruciating headache — the second migraine attack in less than seven days — and went directly to the computer to check the latest Brazilian news, two days after the "biggest popular demonstration against the government in history," my intermittent feeling of alarm was thoroughly justified: After being indicted for the crimes of money-laundering and occultation of assets in the current Brazilian corruption scandal wave, ex-President Lula was invited by the next-in-line-to-be-indicted President Dilma to occupy a high position in office, which would unofficially make him some kind of "non-recognized" Prime Minister, turning Dilma officially into the puppet that she has been for all her time in office, especially in her second term. This would protect Lula from going to trial and maybe to jail as a regular citizen — an arrest warrant was already in the works — but that wasn't the whole story, not even the half of it. With this highly irregular, possibly illegal act, Lula would be elevated to the position of *de facto* leader of Brazil.

According to the media, he had already made his demands: Brazil was supposed to go back in full to the populist and protectionist economic policies that started to destroy the country in the first place; the government should increase spending, and start immediately to "stimulate" the economy, in order to regain its now-tarnished prestige with the poor. Nobody seemed to care that the country was utterly broke, with the highest unemployment rate in many years, inflation on the rise, bankruptcies, companies going out of business, one after the other. Moreover, they couldn't care less about the will of the people, clearly expressed in the huge crowds demonstrating all over the country, a mere two days ago.

The "dictatorship of the P.T. Party[1]" has been (un) officially announced. We were lost.

My last obligation to Brazil was to file my tax returns

---

1 Lula's party, also known as "Worker's Party".

for the year 2015, following the official communication of my change of residency to another country. I had been contemplating asking my accountant to do it on my behalf, and I had time to burn, since the deadline was more than a month ahead. But in light of the latest news, I've decided to do it myself. Immediately. Alan was worried that the new laws concerning the legalization of the assets of Brazilian citizens abroad would affect our own. I guaranteed him this was not "gonna" happen. But the truth is, in Brazil one never knows.

I first tried to download the software into my present computer, but for some mysterious reason it did not work. The software required that I install Java, but apparently this state-of-the-art computer does not allow Java anymore.

I grabbed my old Dell, out of use for a couple of months, but I was so anxious that I did something wrong and managed to provoke the blue screen of death. This time, a permanent one. The computer could not fix itself, and it wouldn't restart. So I tried Alan's computer, a little older than mine, and this one worked.

After half an hour of extreme tension, I completed the forms and sent them directly to the Ministry of Finance through the Internet. I saved and printed the confirmation receipt — the tax report system in Brazil is pretty advanced — and I was done.

I had been by myself through all this "little" personal crisis, since Alan had gone to the dentist. So I took a deep breath, put on my snickers and leggings, and went for a run at the gym, facing the pool and the newly-flowered dogwood trees announcing the imminent spring. I was far from home and suffering from the occasional longing. But I was safe and sound.

Now, as I finish writing this chronicle, Lula's confirmation as a Minister of State has been put on hold until later today, or maybe tomorrow, because a greater scandal has taken place: It was confirmed that another minister of state belonging to P.T., the Worker's Party, tried to obstruct justice by bribing a senator to derail the man's plea bargain, the same senator who brought proof against Lula and Dilma to the corruption trial. Lula does not want to share the headlines with lesser criminals than himself, the indisputable chief of the gang, the "intellectual" mentor of Brazil's demise.

***

When this chronicle finally aired on Saturday morning, Lula's confirmation was swaying back and forth according to the determinations of the Supreme Court.

The Brazilian people are clearly against it, but the "gang in office" does not care at all. Their rudeness, their profound contempt for the people and for the Law is ostensibly made manifest by the vulgarity of their language and their even more vulgar contentions, in a total disregard for the Constitution made public by Sergio Moro — the judge in charge of "*Lava-Jato*" [Carwash], as we dubbed the corruption trials — through the wiretapped conversations between the most important officials in the country. How shocking.

It doesn't matter. What matters is that, at this moment, we all know for sure something we had just suspected for so many years: There is indeed a "gang in office," and that certainty constitutes an important step in our struggle to get rid of them.

Enough is enough.

THE CREAM THERMOS AT STARBUCKS

I t was Sunday morning, the first Sunday of spring in Greenville, SC.

I had just received an email containing a much-awaited feedback response from a newspaper. It was negative. I was disappointed.

Oh well. Being an adult, I had no right to be so utterly distressed over another broken dream. I had a husband to attend to, therefore I asked Alan if he would like to go out for breakfast.

In all honesty, if I merely intended to go on living, a radical change was in order. I just didn't know where to start. Maybe going out for breakfast on a spring Sunday. Maybe no longer writing about my persistent failures, or starting to focus on being "successful."

I could certainly tell you, that is, tell my readers outside the U.S., how stunning the beginning of springtime in this country is. There are fresh strokes of color all over the place, as if a talented painter had just woken up and put his hands to work. "Nature," some would say. Maybe "God." Uplifting, from every angle you look at it.

We drove to our favorite breakfast joint, a 5-minute

drive from our house. House, not home. "I hate this house," Alan had just admitted, reminding me of Caetano Veloso, a famous Brazilian song-writer who once wrote: "I want to set this apartment on fire, but you don't believe me." I was inclined to agree. I hated it as well. We've lived here too long.

The breakfast place was packed, it had a half-hour wait. It might have been too late for breakfast; or, on the other hand, it was the exact time of the day for people who attend church, the vast majority in this neck of the woods, dubbed "the Bible Belt." Chances were other restaurants would also be crowded, so we postponed coffee for a while and drove to our property, which we're supposed to visit a couple of days a week in order to imagine how great it will feel to be living up there. Which is expected to happen, eventually.

I confess I don't have a clue about the rules to achieve success. At any rate, there is an overabundance of efficient recipes out there to follow if we are seriously planning to join the "happy few," although I feel strongly it is failure that makes us human, or binds us closer to people who are "just human." Olympus is somewhere else. Anointed gods don't act like the average Joe, and, moreover, they are surely aware of a couple of sacred tricks they don't wish to share, despite the millions of dollars spent and earned through publishing books on this subject matter.

But I digress. On our way down from Paris Mountain, we decided to stop at the Starbucks near the supermarket. At first sight, since it's located in a parking lot, it looks like a desolated coffee shop at a random gas station. But as you enter, it's a Starbucks, with the exact same color scheme and layout as any other Starbucks anywhere in the world. I wonder if this highly planned uniformity is the secret to business success; I might add that coffee at Starbucks is always great, although the food might not be so extraordinary.

What I loathe about Starbucks is that, no matter where you are, in Rio de Janeiro or in Paris or in L.A., it is necessary to know exactly what is demanded of you in order to reach the desired results, no manual of instructions added. Therefore, after I grabbed Alan's cup and mine — Alan was waiting for the food — I went straight to the cream & sugar counter and discovered that the cream thermos was practically empty. Trying to act like an insider, I pointed it out to the girl behind the coffee counter, and went even further, taking the empty thermos and leaving it right in front of her, before heading back to my seat.

There was a copy of *The New York Times* lying on the table, and Alan started to read it with genuine interest, something I was repeatedly failing to understand. Less than an hour ago he has been harshly criticizing the same newspaper for its political stance, and for all the "lies" they publish every day. I was in no position to remind him, or myself, of how relevant I believed the paper still was. Especially on this spring Sunday morning, when I had been rejected for the nth time.

I needed some urgent distraction from my negative thoughts, so I began to observe my fellow customers, while my mind simultaneously wandered through my past, summing up what I have accomplished so far. Although, of course, having changed my course so violently by leaving behind my own country, my chances of reaping positive results were now remarkably slim. For whatever life I have left, I will never be able to fit in.

The cream thermos was still on the counter, exactly where I'd left it, untouched. Alan — who, to his utmost relief, is now home after his own self-imposed exile — undoubtedly knew the right path to the cream and how to pour it in his coffee, while the best I could come up with was asking the wrong person to fill the wrong thermos by putting it in the wrong place.

In my mental musings, I started to reflect about the Trump phenomenon and the crowds that were following the presidential candidate, widely qualified in the mainstream media as a herd of misfits, illiterate, "disposable" people. I caught the impeccable irony implied in the fact that a successful billionaire, possibly an obstinate reader of Hitler's unrestrained speeches — as Alan and I had discussed earlier, based on an article published in *The New York Times* — surprisingly managed to find his way into the hearts of such a dispossessed, boisterous, demanding mob. Or for this very reason: his inflamed rhetoric.

Alan kindly offered me solace on that dreary spring morning, advising that I should simply surrender. There was no way I could make myself known as a writer in the highly competitive English-speaking world, among a myriad of outstanding natives coming out of Ivy League universities. Perhaps I should limit myself to my native Portuguese, keep myself contained within the modest circle of third-world admirers I have already amassed, stop "courting people who do not appreciate me and learn to accept those who do." In other words, I'd better make my life easier and go easy on myself, stop aiming for the sky (and start focusing on my grave, I was tempted to add).

Alright. Time for a well-deserved break.

"I can feel you want to leave," Alan said, putting aside *The Times Book Review*. He threw the empty cups into the garbage bin next to our table, and we walked to the door. The cream thermos rested untouched on the coffee counter, and I bet it was going to stay that way until the night janitor finally came to clean up the place, a foreign worker, probably.

The Bathroom Craze

First of all, let me make myself clear: I have no problem whatsoever with sharing the bathroom with a male, provided he's clean and thoughtful, and skillfully manages the delicate toilet seat issue. Which, luckily enough, is my case here at home. Now, if we have the slightest intention of mingling public toilets in the future, I strongly advise the establishment of a significant penalty to avoid possible misdemeanors like this one, and we'd be all set. I would not mind at all the elimination of this kind of old-fashioned bathroom prejudice, which has ended up being such a disturbing issue lately.

Now, since we've chosen to settle down in South Carolina, a mere 20-mile drive from the North Carolina border, I guess this might turn us into borderline fascist pigs, oops, sorry, pigs. It does not matter we moved here because our son lives in Charleston, or because Greenville is a city on the rise, with a highly-praised quality of life. What's essential is that North Carolina's governor is a bigot, a despicable monster who hates gays — yes, I chose this hateful, highly prejudiced term (or is it not?) for a reason. You may speculate on this, I don't care. In terms of the governor, I assume by now it's common knowledge that he has just passed legislation forbidding transgender people from using the bathroom assigned to the gender they are aspiring to, or at least that's what I have understood. But I could be wrong, since it could be just the opposite, right? We must agree this is a quite controversial subject for everyone involved, and also for us, non-LGBT outsiders.

In fact, any conclusion in this prejudiced direction would be utterly mistaken, since I consider myself reasonably open and willing to respect other people's individuality, provided it does not affect my own. This would also include, of course, some level of tolerance toward opposing political views. In my intimate circle of family and friends, for example, we range from conservatives to Bernie Sanders supporters (not me, not yet), passing through various degrees of moderation.

Now, if you believe the U.S. at this moment to be a highly-polarized country, you should know what's happening back in Brazil, where people on opposite sides are perilously on the verge of direct confrontation. Which, on a personal note, is not the worst. Take, for example, three people whom I greatly admired in the past, some sort of literary mentors, if I may say so. One of them ended up publicly opposing the State of Israel based solely upon widely spread propaganda slogans and a B.D.S ruling; another has just positioned himself strongly in favor of the P.T. Party, which is now struggling to discredit the judicial proof of a deeply ingrained network of kickbacks and other corrupt practices that had been established as a norm for government institutions. So far, this has resulted in an unprecedented economic, political and moral crisis that, according to *The Washington Times*, places Brazil "on the brink of unraveling," with no solution in sight. I felt so sad concerning my former friends' standpoints that I would have a hard time describing what happened without falling into a depressive episode, aggravated by my feelings of inadequacy and inability to react in a way that could show them how wrong they are.

This reminds me of a dream I had more than 40 years ago, shortly after my father's premature death. I had taken a relative to the airport and was driving on a straight, clear highway, heading home. Suddenly, a huge truck came up from the opposite direction, sporting a "Do Not Enter" sign in place of the rear-view mirror. Not by coincidence, that's the exact description of how my father died, in a car accident, hit by a truck coming from the opposite direction operated by a drunk driver. In my dream, I was then stopped by a policeman in a French Revolution uniform, who told me to step out of the car. He asked me if "I had a child or a sick person to take care of." I knew the answer was "no," but felt so confused that I was unable to utter the word, and began to cry instead.

Back to real life. Interestingly enough, my third friend came up this week with a description of how he's been facing his own friends, who, like the one I mentioned above, show unjustifiable support for the Brazilian government and officials who have been accused of corruption and money-laundering crimes, among other things. I was surprised, and also emotional, because it was so close to my dream of the past. My friend also accused ex-president Lula of being responsible for forcing him into the right against his will, a crime he found himself incapable of forgiving. And so do I. Fortunately, my 24-year-old nephew told me the other day that, although political discussions are pretty violent on Facebook, in real life people rarely mention this topic, limiting themselves to drinking and having fun.

Therefore, it might not be coincidental that I've un-consciously chosen to live in a conservative state, although I totally ignored this fact when we bought the proper-ty on Paris Mountain. All I was tempted to consider was the beautiful view, the proximity to our son, and the nice friendly weather for most of the year. Blame me if you will.

Honestly, even if it's not fair to be stealing a slogan from the latest terrorist attack in Belgium — a much more painful situation — *moi aussi, je suis* sick of this state of af-fairs. Not to mention a priest was allegedly crucified in the caliphate on Good Friday. Or maybe he wasn't.

In my daily life, I actually praise diversity: I have to confess, for example, that I eat cereal at night, before going to sleep, so what. And I won't even dare accuse a particular group of immigrants for making a mess in our condomini-um's laundromat, since I have not caught them in the act yet. It could well be a Brazilian like myself, right? Though I've never met one around here.

As for my own "immigrant status," I seem to be get-ting a thicker skin, finally. This Spring, at least, I was spared the allergic reaction that was terribly disturbing last year, my first on U.S. soil.

In Defense of Donald Trump
(Or Not so Much)

Okay. What I write does not matter, at least to the powers that be or whoever supports them. However, although it will probably be a day late and a dollar short when it's finally published, a few days after the Wisconsin primary, this article is a very serious one, prompted by a provocative article in *Tablet Magazine*, which affirmed there is a complete absence of serious articles in favor of Donald Trump — meaning, the candidate is indefensible by serious, conscious people. Moreover, like most other articles on the subject, *Tablet* lumps all Trump supporters together in the same pot, a pot filled to the top with reactionary, racist, illiterate, ignorant people, who, apparently, are more abundant in the United States than we previously thought. And that's where I come in.

First, I must tell you where I'm coming from. In my country, Brazil, which, thanks to its very serious crisis made the front page of *The New York Times* this week, people like me, despite being the vast majority at this moment, are being publicly discredited by the so-called "intellectuals" — in our case, writers, artists and other opinionated personalities who favor the P.T. Party, preferably dubbed "Worker's Party" in the U.S. media. These people, whose righteousness sounds authoritarian to the point of being offensive, and of ignoring everybody else's ideas as despicable and invalid, have been closing their eyes to the obvious criminal behavior of their all-time favorites. And lo and behold, these supporters line up side by side with the government in the helping-the-poor fallacy, the fairness of which apparently justifies any hideous lie: Among so many popular myths — which, on the other hand, are quite unpopular today — the most audacious one is about them having improved the life conditions of the Brazilian poor. How are "their" poor faring right now? A deeper look will certainly tell.

There's no doubt the right side is the side of the poor, of the destitute, against the rich and privileged. But what happens when those who were supposed to help, and had the power to do so, used their policies as a mask to fill their own self-fulfilling pockets, at the expense of everybody else? Where did the proverbial fairness of the left go, in this case? And what if, like is now happening in Brazil, these policies result in a wrecked country? How can the poor do well in such a disgraceful status quo?

This has nothing to do with the present situation in the U.S., of course. And yet, it does. We, serious people who don't have a say, and don't make the opinion page of *The New York Times*, are an island of shaken ideas surrounded on all sides by noisy, "correct lies."

Donald Trump may not lie. But I believe he does. Only, unlike his opponents, he has chosen a far more dangerous, yet surprisingly successful, path: Instead of misleading us with the so-called correct lies, he co-opts many of us with his sincere-sounding half-truths, connecting on a much more personal level when compared to the more obvious, theoretical fairness of the "selfless, flawless behavior" of other politicians, which is, in most part, blatantly false.

Take the abortion issue, for example, one of the worst *faux pas* of Trump's campaign so far, which has seemingly set him on a self-destruction course. It is quite clear for those who have eyes and ears that Trump is in fact pro-choice. But he must have been told that if he wanted to count as a good conservative, and thus win votes, this dog would not hunt. Therefore, he flipped, without giving it too much thought: *I'll say it, that's it. I don't need to believe it!* And yet he was caught, not by a smarter opponent, but by an attentive reporter who was better prepared for the situation at hand.

Is it excusable to say on the air that, "in case abortion is made illegal, women should be punished for it?" No! Women should be treated like the spoiled little pets they are, protected like an endangered species. Therefore, *in the hypothetical case* in which abortion is ruled unlawful, which is quite unlikely, women should not be deemed responsible for their own choices or actions. After all, I was told most U.S. women are incapable of controlling their own reproduction traits, much less protecting themselves from unwanted pregnancies through the many means at their disposal today. Now, *this* would be the correct answer: Women must learn to protect themselves. Period.

Although most of the blustering claims we hear from candidates are mostly unviable, and their ideas unpractical, we are still subject to judgmental reactions when criticizing those who "sound" fair, palatable, like Bernie Sanders, for example. A friend in Brazil, who maintains her stance as the eternal hippie, was all excited around him: "This candidate is the one who fits best in the new world order," she said. What does she know?

I used to trust (and admire) the United States as a country under the rule of Law, in which democracy thrives and the Congress counts. But what do I know: Obama's multiple executive orders have proven this is not always the case. Therefore, the president does matter, and that's why I have the most doubts about whether to back Trump or not. He certainly does not "seem" presidential to me, at least *not yet*. Nevertheless, he declared last Sunday in an interview: "I can act presidential if I want. I will act so presidential you will find me boring," he said; and therein lies the rub, the danger: By telling the truth on this rare occasion, he had just confessed that he lies most of the time, like everybody else does in the present presidential race...

At any rate, those who see some level of value in Donald Trump's candidacy, and who, on the other hand, *see themselves as good and fair* (the bad and the ugly do not care about other people's opinion) are so overwhelmed by his opponents' propaganda they don't dare to talk or write about their real impressions.

A curious case was that of an allegedly honest, sincere, well-intentioned veteran, who began his article published in *The New York Times* listing myriad reasons why people, like himself and his family, should support Donald Trump based on what the candidate says in his rallies — against war and in favor of justifiable anger, for example. "He torments a G.O.P. elite that cannot admit its own failures," the veteran writes. And yet he concludes by affirming that "Donald Trump is unfit for our nation's highest office." Why? He does not say. Maybe somebody told him so, or he *knows what he's supposed to say* to be praised, accepted; and published, which is important. But he honestly ignores the real reason behind it.

What I would truly like to hear, before I finally make

my move to offer my (totally useless) support to any candidate in this electoral race, is a little bit of quiet, a little bit of truth, a little bit of unbiased common sense. Which is too much to ask, I know. It's not likely to happen. Good luck with that.

Therefore, if, God forbid, things go awry, Donald Trump gets elected president and ends up being the new Hitler people expect him to be, I will willingly take my share of the blame, apologizing on Facebook for putting these horrible thoughts on paper. And I'll do it immediately, I promise.

The Day After

"What are you going to do tomorrow?" Alan asked me, at four in the morning, during one of our regular insomnia episodes.

I answer him distractedly, while at the same time sliding my thumb over the surface of my cell phone to check the latest Facebook posts from Brazil: I'll try to make a video-release for one of my authors; I'll work a little on the house project; I'll finally begin to translate my novel into English, which is my next professional assignment; nothing; nada. I'm not doing anything at all. I'll just keep myself alert.

I'm in a total state of alertness. I'm actually so alert that I almost passed up on my weekly obligation to write, which I ended up fulfilling anyway, thanks to habit, to the utmost relief brought by the writing practice. I've been very active on the political forum created by Brazilians on Facebook to discuss the upcoming impeachment of our president, keeping the energy high all week to avoid indulging in depression and lethargy.

To tell you the truth, I've been living in a state of "suspended animation," or better said, divided, not only between two countries, but also between two different states of mind: While staying committed to previously assigned projects, and some urgent, unpostponable decisions, a good percentage of my mind is occupied by the Brazilian political situation and the impeachment process results.

Although I don't have to confront the Brazilian reality on a daily basis, facing, as a friend told me, "the empty streets, because people lack the basic money even for a bus ticket over the weekend," or witnessing in person the absurdity of an Esplanada — the impressive avenue in Brasilia, lined with government buildings, and with the National Congress at its apex — artificially divided by metal barriers, I still feel as if I were physically present in Brazil. After almost two years of self-exile, I still find myself incapable of truly feeling that "I'm not in Kansas anymore," I mean, in Itaipava. If I were actually there, despite the loud rumors of a "coup" I would probably enjoy a peaceful weekend, including a delicious lunch in the brand-new Pizzeria Matilda, which belongs to a friend of mine. Yeah, right. Maybe. On the other hand, it would be much more difficult to figure out some kind of solution to daily survival, as I would probably be part of the growing unemployed and hopeless mob, who knows.

Meanwhile, my physical body, together with the available percentage of my brain, keeps developing the 5th or 6th version of our Paris Mountain house architectural plans. The one completed by a professional, well-paid architect, actually proved unbuildable — oh, yes, con artists are not exclusive to the Brazilian way of life. Moreover, we can now count on the support of a benevolent builder, although I'm staying skeptical in order to avoid the evil eye.

We are in need of a benevolent builder, that is correct, one who is willing to accept our clean, logical, simple and fluid house plans, which apparently go very much against the local neo-rococo style, insisting instead on the impractical Bauhaus slogan "form follows function." We've already been rejected by three or four other builders... Who could imagine we would end up missing our Brazilian contractor, and the construction guarantee "based on his mustache"?

It is my belief that, thanks to the detailed simplicity we are theoretically seeking, builders must unrealistically conclude their percentage won't be enough to fulfill their first-world ambitions, who knows. Nobody in the United States wants to work for a small amount of money, or solely for the love, the excitement of the job; nobody wants to be an "amateur," as one could say (from Latin, *amator*, *amare*). This could eventually change, if, by chance, Bernie Sanders was elected president, right? Not really. I'm not supporting him at all, as after the Brazilian experience I'm done with government leftism for whatever life I have left.

According to Alan, everybody has a family to support and a mortgage to pay. Which would, obviously, include the blunt, insistent telemarketers who call us all the time. *Caramba*! You can't solicit any information in this country without eliciting endless, unwanted phone calls! Indeed, you need a high level of wariness to protect yourself from these "slaves of percentage," something I had previously ignored. The other day, for instance, while looking for English courses, I was naïve enough to provide my personal data to a college network, *et voilà*, now they never stop calling. I was forced to drop the search for a better car insurance because I refused to fill out a number of forms with my actual information.

However, my worst experience was still to come, when I gave in to an emphatic invitation from LinkedIn to apply for an "Outstanding Professional Women's Award" or something, which at some point, I believed, could help me find my way in the U.S.

How gullible of me. It was early one morning when I got the call from New York. A pretty persuasive woman informed me that my application has been "accepted," but to confirm it, she would need to proceed with a 15-minute interview (if this number reminds you of something, it is not coincidental).

"Go ahead," I said.

It was like giving her my head on a plate. *Let's see how far will this go*, I told myself. And while the woman used me to fulfill her percentage expectations, I used her to lift up my deeply affected exile self-esteem. I proceeded to tell her in detail my remarkable trajectory as an e-book pioneer in Brazil, the old, useless tale I'm so tired of telling everybody, whenever I can. At the same time, I couldn't stop thinking about the present situation in Brazil, where everything I might have ever accomplished was torn to shreds — once again. It did not get any easier, even if compared to the urgency of the moment.

My "15 minutes" ended abruptly when the woman tried to charge me $900 for a lifetime membership, quickly replaced by a cheaper 5-year one, to end up melancholically with $150 for a one-year trial, which I also refused. When I told her I would call her back, she grew suddenly mad, almost yelling at me seconds before hanging up on me, destroying all of her previous dedicated efforts to build up confidence: "Didn't you read the membership rules before applying?"

Honestly, I'd tried. But I couldn't find anything about fees in the convoluted form, carefully designed to fool needy people, eager for some recognition, easy targets for this kind of advertising "ambush."

Our ideal networked reality is being made into a virtual jungle, my friends, one that outdoes, with its unsuspected creative virulence, the sad corruption on the Brazilian political scene. Today, on the eve of the vote for impeachment in the Brazilian Congress, I keep counting vote by vote, trying not to consider the possibility of defeat, so great is the envisioned relief if impeachment is approved at last, notwithstanding the future challenges we might be faced with, in order to maintain democracy on its proper tracks.

Time to invoke our daily Churchill to support us a bit: "Democracy is the worst form of government, except for all the others." It is hard to imagine there are still some people who accuse us of perpetrating a political coup, using the lowest of arguments and moral lynching in order to convince us of their failed notions around pristine social justice. Just minutes ago, I read an "intellectual" statement affirming that ex-president Lula is "the biggest Brazilian leader alive today," and there's no reason to "submit to an illegitimate government." Illegitimate, yes, though backed by Congress and the Supreme Court, not to mention the weight of popular support.

On the personal side, I've developed a profound disgust regarding ex-president Lula. Last night, when he appeared on BBC News while I was running on the treadmill, I was forced to avert my eyes, something which has only happened to me in two other occasions: when I was a child, watching *The Ten Commandments*, in order to avoid the leper's scene, as advised by my mother; and whenever I see someone injecting themselves with heroin or crack — free association allowed.

Less than 24 hours from now, we might be facing an entirely new set of circumstances in Brazil, and I'm ardently anticipating it. There may be lots of garbage, lots of dust clouding the way, but still, for the first time in our history, we won't be sweeping it under the rug, and this *per se* will make the air more breathable.

Little by little, we will recover the capacity for a whole night's sleep; we will have our lives back, lives rudely taken from us by the criminal nerve of this odious character who will soon be behind bars, God willing. And I'm sure God will, at least to prove He was "born in Brazil," like Brazilians once dared to believe.

THOUGH LOVE

It's been four years this week that my mother died, after a long struggle against alzheimer's disease (no capitals, please).

I still hurt. I still remember, as if it were today, her harsh comments, probably reflecting her deepest fears that I and my brother really "hated" her. A baseless fear, since, despite our sometimes-rough relationship with her, both he and I took good care of her up to the last moments. Which is not always the case, as we well know. A person I know went to New York on holiday, hours after her mother had a life-threatening stroke and was admitted to the hospital. Others believe they have no obligation whatsoever to take care of their elderly parents, even advising others in this direction, as I've read recently on a blog.

My mother was tough. Yet, I have no doubt about her motherly love — although she loved my brother more, of course, as is the rule in Jewish families. Just kidding.

At any rate, the brain has this property of playing (bad) tricks on us. Therefore, due to some kind of disease, or under the influence of specific drugs, we may end up mistreating the people we love the most, and that deeply love us back. No harm intended. Yet harm is done.

It happened to me again this week, and it's happening still. My husband, who regularly takes a sleeping pill, has fallen victim of a bad drug interaction due to a dental implant procedure. He was anticipating the surgery and highly anxious about it, which is understandable. Not only his looks, but also his ability to bite were under serious risk, not because of old age or anything like that, but due to the fracturing of an old root, which released an outdated crown. The tooth had in fact been lost in a bike accident when he was a child; but at our age, these kinds of events are always disturbing — a threat, a fearful announcement that life is about to end at some point. Therefore, when he added a strong sedative and an equally strong painkiller, both prescribed by the surgeon, to his usual "drug recipe," the result was disastrous. He fell victim of a psychotic episode and has been awake for three nights, talking to himself, almost delirious, with very brief intervals of consciousness. I've seen a few damaged brains in this life, and have dealt with them; but I couldn't find my strength, when, before figuring out what the actual situation was, I suspected my husband to have alzheimer's, just like my mother before him.

Relief came partially and subtly when I discovered the unintended mixing of prescription drugs, so now I'm hoping for a fast recovery, as signaled by yesterday's brief episode of consciousness, before he indulged in a larger-than-usual dosage of his regular sleeping aid, *et voilà*, psychosis took him over once again. And of course, the target of his rage was, as I said before, the person he loves the most (according to my utmost hope), and who loves him back.

I've had a lot on my plate lately. In addition to my daily worries, my country, Brazil, is undergoing a serious crisis, the culprit of which, albeit an alleged "victim," is under the influence of heavy medication and has been acting erratically. The old brain playing its tricks! It's not a surprise that, as President Dilma reacts, she not only reflects her complete oblivion to her obligations as "mother of the nation," but also a hateful contempt of her people's well-being. Maybe the improper target of her rage is... etc., etc.

I'm very aware that, to a certain extent, outside issues can be embraced as a reflection of our own personal pain. Which would explain, for example, why I have been so invested in writing about Brazilian politics — or American politics, by the way — due to my own internal workings or eventual trauma. I should know better, and get a life! But could that be also true of more than 100 million people (56% of Brazilian population) at the same time? Unlikely!

Back to "motherly love." Only recently, as you all know, I started to consider myself a mother and put to work my motherly loving resources. Therefore, I was deeply in doubt if I was supposed to congratulate my son, who was recently accepted as a lawyer to the Marine Corps. His friends were delighted. His fiancée was proud. But, honestly, as a mother, although I could also be proud of him if I tried harder, I was afraid, concerned about his safety. What could I do? Lie to him? I decided to simply tell the truth, as is my regular style, my own truth, at least — tough love, the kind of love that just tells the truth, which can be painful, and usually is. Tough love has been lacking in our networked civilization, where everybody is seeking approval, and it is common sense that we should grant it.

I believe the imposition of a "progressive" agenda to be part of this picture. Take, for instance, this widely expressed (and overrated) support for "transgender bathroom rights," something that disturbs me so deeply I already wrote about it a couple of weeks ago. In all honesty, how many transgender people — a recognizably rare condition — can exist in this world? In this country? In our town?

Before my personal and national hell broke loose, I was very impressed by a movie I watched last week, *The Danish Girl*, which depicts the first case of a transgender woman (or man?) to subject herself, himself, to "sex reassignment surgery," or something like that. Einar Wegener (a superb Eddie Redmayne) was a happy young painter, a married man who loved his young wife dearly, or so it seemed. Things started to get a little crazy when this young woman, who was also a painter, asked him to pose for a painting dressed as a girl.

The situation rapidly evolved from an isolated cross-dressing funny episode to Wegener starting to believe he was "internally" a woman, and acting on it. There's an impressive scene when he skillfully hides his beautiful penis (sorry, I couldn't resist) between his legs, while trying to act "feminine" in front of a mirror in a theater dressing room. What bothered me the most was the fact that, instead of trying to stop him — tough love — his loving wife and a few other friends ostensibly encouraged him.

Lili, the "new woman" — it is a true story, and Lili Elbe is considered today a "pioneer," and a kind of heroic figure for the transgender movement — decided to undergo a series of increasingly dangerous (and untested) "corrective" surgeries.

Consequently, not only the beautiful penis was dead and gone. According to Lili's and her doctor's ambitions, as she wanted to "have children," besides attempting to create a fake vagina, the doctor — a true harbinger of Dr. Mengele — also tried to transplant a uterus.

The patient died.

I don't care, as the movie's critics were eager to point out, if the story lacks many details and ultimately fails to be faithful to the facts. What was painful to watch was the "new woman" trying to kill the man (now) inside her, as well as his art. Since being a successful painter was part of "him," but not of "her," she decides to work as a shop girl, while waiting on his/ her long-planned painful suicide. And that I could not forgive.

I remember my mother's desperation when I got involved with a gay man, a long time ago. She yelled at me, doubted my judgment, and I was so angry at her! How could she be so insensitive, so disrespectful toward my feelings? Tough love. She was right. I suffered a lot.

Now imagine how many loving, respectful parents are currently encouraging their children's "gender discomfort," giving them dangerous drugs, and ultimately providing mutilating surgery?

I confess: As a teenager, I had a few sexual doubts myself. Treacherous brain. It took me a long time to menstruate. My breasts were nonexistent at an "advanced" age. Later, at the beginning of my professional life as an architect and furniture designer, I was considered too bold, too daring, to be a "woman." I failed repeatedly to recognize some femininity in me, to the point of making myself incapable of a true orgasm. Imagine what a recipe for disaster this would be, with today's permissiveness.

I needed a lot of patience, resilience and persistence until, after a number of failed relationships, I found my husband Alan on the Internet and could finally orgasm, at 53 years old. After that, not only did my vagina prove very active and effective, but even my breasts grew big, impressively big.

I apologize for my "masculine" bluntness in this chronicle, my friends, but I'm sure you'll understand. Today, after all, people feel free to expose their own sexual idiosyncrasies to the utmost detail, correct? And please remember: Tough love is a lot better than no love at all, or a crooked love, which responds to progressive propaganda and fails to do what is truly right. It can most certainly save lives.

I SUPPORT DONALD TRUMP FOR PRESIDENT OF THE UNITED STATES

It is no use trying to sum people up. One must follow hints, not exactly what is said, nor yet entirely what is done.

Virginia Woolf

The day has finally arrived, and there's no easy way to say this: I decided to support Donald Trump as candidate for President of the United States.

I know that by doing this I risk losing a few Facebook friends, and maybe some clients. So be it. I can take it. And I don't plan to do this, as has happened lately, by affirming the negative issues or pointing out the negative qualities in other candidates. After all, I'm totally entitled to my own opinion, something I've learned the hard way in the last few weeks of Brazilian political turmoil.

If people can declare that they "followed their heart" when voting for Bernie Sanders in the New York primaries, for example, why can't I do the same? Who died and left any of them king? King of the "right opinion," at least? Owners of the "ultimate truth"?

Let's face it: There's no "ultimate truth" involved in politics. It's all theater. And our role in this impossible guessing game is to try to see behind the smoke screens both sides have dedicated themselves to blowing in our way on a daily basis.

As I'm writing on Wednesday, after five Trump victories in the latest primaries, it might seem "evident" that I'm opting for the indisputable front-runner on the Republican side, assuming that the "Republican option" is something I chose a long time ago, when I first grew disappointed with Barack Obama after rooting for him so strongly. Or after I decided to give in to the remarkable pressure my husband exerts on me, except that I recognize he has actually convinced me through reasonable, logical arguments.

There's no point in highlighting failed reasoning, such as "nobody can be elected President of the United States without winning Ohio." I could react: Nobody can be elected President of the United States by *only* winning Ohio, don't you agree? I also fail to see the point in emphasizing Ted Cruz's attempt to solve this riddle by putting himself and Kasich together on a team of losers, thus "pretending" Cruz — or the newly-created double entity — has won Ohio, and is, therefore, entitled to the presidency, in a twisted rationale. Or, after this deal was quickly deemed unfeasible, pretending to be the Republican nominee by appointing two-percent Fiorina, "singing" Fiorina, as his "vice-president."

Ted Cruz: What a frightening character. And yet I saw myself compared to him in a pretty unfair response to my positions, expressed in a comment in *The New York Times*. Too timely to be considered something other than a fortuitous coincidence — I don't believe in coincidences, *pero que las hay, las hay* — I was confronted with a Modern Love article on the very day I've published my previous chronicle "Tough Love," which was, more or less, about the same subject — "the transgender mania," oops, sorry, "movement." I did not hesitate one minute before trying to enter *The New York Times* "arena" through the back door, that is, by posting a link to my chronicle in a comment.

It worked: A few people more than the usual couple of readers were redirected to my published essay. Fortunately, the vast majority of comments to *The New York Times* article followed the same line of reasoning mine did, reflecting a clear rejection of an obvious minority's imposing views, which have been given a privileged podium by an equally imposing "leftist agenda," or something in this direction.

Not only was I compared to Ted Cruz, but I was also contemptuously qualified as a "cisgender" — for those of you who still don't know what the term means, it refers to "a person whose gender option equals the gender assigned at birth," something deeply *offensive*, apparently. Why should I — or anyone, for that matter — be subjected to such a limiting fate? Forced to accept that I'm a woman, just because I was born one? When has nature ever been assigned such an indisputable, anti-democratic role?

Despite the (positive) fact that I was forced to accept how hard it is to adopt the role of a commentator in these extremist days — it takes a "thick skin," indeed — I was also happy to learn not everybody has finally lost their senses. A good number of women tried to explain how, for instance, their breasts (and mine!) are a living, nourishing element, intertwined with blood vessels, nerve terminals and the like, not a mere "sack filled with fluid." One gay man stated a unique point of view, according to which the "transgender movement" is actually a retrogression, going in the opposite direction of earlier sexual freedom demands and their consequential gains. "Biological sex is not changeable," he said. "Transgenderism is rooted in regressive ideas of what it means to be male and female."

Now, you could surely ask, what the heck has this gender frenzy to do with Donald Trump being elected president?

What I believe is that the already mentioned "leftist agenda" has lost its way. What started as a defense of fundamental human rights, joyously supported by our generation in our younger years, has degenerated into a kind of "dictatorship of the minorities." And I'm not trying to dismiss real, crucial human rights, such as the freedom of speech, of expression, or even more crucial, the right to a home, enough food, money and education to enable a fair quality of life. Neither do I mean to describe actual "minorities," such as the poor, or people of (other than white) color, or, imagine that, "women" — clarifying the ironic quotation marks: according to nature, women should account for about 50% of the human race — but actual "rarities." Why should we let ourselves be limited, utterly abused by these rarest of beings, to satisfy their utmost convenience?

Don't get me wrong. As a "recent conservative," I'm in favor of everybody's freedom. As long as it does not interfere with my own.

This does not mean that, once elected, Donald Trump will be able to stop this maddening trend, or even be interested in stopping it. But I'm sure Hillary Clinton will do her best to maintain it, as shown in her speeches, in which LGBT — Lesbian, Gay, Bisexual and Transgender — rights are always highlighted. Or even if she doesn't, the actual election of a Democrat, a so-called "liberal," will send a powerful message that we, the majority, endorse this nonsense, this overwhelming loss of reason that is prevailing at this moment.

As I write, I am listening, without paying too much attention, to Donald Trump's "major foreign policy speech." Nothing really new on that front, pardon the unintentional pun. Whatever he says or does at this point, we must understand what is at stake: a presidential election; votes; period. Radical national movements or changes in this country's international course, although depending on the president's style as previously seen, still have to be approved by a Congress and a Senate, right?

We are deeply in need of a change; that is a fact. It does not mean that, no matter how hard we try, we will be able to cross the thick smoke screen that conceals the future in order to envision the right direction. All we can rely on is our internal (moral) compass, which may be seriously damaged today by the intensity of so many different opinions attacking us from all kinds of networks, reflecting all kinds of disguised prejudice, intolerance, and usually undeserved, yet emphatic affirmations. This is a world in which the loudest voice, or at least the one with most "likes," is taken as the right one.

I will limit myself to endorsing Donald Trump for two reasons (and of course I'm being ironic): Firstly, like him, I like to nickname people; and secondly, I always begin a much-anticipated revelation by saying "I would never say that..." followed by that very thing I would never say. If I'm horribly wrong, we will soon find out. Or not, in case Hillary is elected. Ultimately, there is no such thing as "if." I'm just following my best instincts. Period. There's no point in contradicting them, at least for me.

Not to mention, of course, that the majority of issues or talking points in this election season were introduced by Donald Trump at the very beginning, if you already forgot or failed to pay attention. The others have been limiting themselves to parroting him, or arguing against his ideas, with few exceptions. Which means, Donald Trump is already the "brain" behind the future government, the one dealing the cards, although Alan has criticized him for being unable to read on a teleprompter.

Now that the "big speech" is over, there's no comparing Obama's charisma to Donald Trump's. It is a fact. Time will tell if great charisma is really what we need to make this world better. We started so well on the greater justice and fairness path, a few years ago. Where did we lose ourselves on the way?

Maybe we will fare better if we opt for a not so "clear" notion of what is right. I currently do not know. I would certainly be happier to make this "endorsement" in a more excited, righteous tone, like our opponents usually do. I cannot. The world does not allow me, since I'm still in doubt about so many issues, so many choices; but not concerning this one. This one is said and done.

FEED THE GOOD

Not that I did not know it, since all these facts put together have affected me personally in such a profound way, but I wasn't really "aware" of it until I read about it on Wednesday morning in Thomas Friedman's column in *The New York Times*: "In 2007, Apple came out with the iPhone, beginning the smartphone/ apps revolution; in late 2006 Facebook opened its doors to anyone, not just college and high school students, and took off like a rocket; Google came out with the Android operating system in 2007; [...] Amazon came out with the Kindle in 2007." As I have affirmed so many times, KBR, the publishing company I started in Brazil in 2008, was based upon the Kindle to such an extent that is was originally named "KindleBookBr," until Amazon asked us to change it. Just for the record, the "K" in "KBR" still accounts for our beloved "Kindle," no need to explain the "BR."

It's not difficult to figure out how this technological surge has affected other people, particularly in the U.S., where all these "novelties" were created, encouraged and adopted in a heartbeat. I remember the debate after Obama's first election in 2008, about whether or not to "allow" him to keep his Blackberry as president. Can anyone imagine such a discussion today?

Blackberries are long gone, and technology is still considered an enemy of sorts in third-world countries, such as Brazil (sorry, folks), where this very week WhatsApp was blocked by a judge for 72 hours, because the company refused to deliver information it didn't even have access to. I wasn't surprised to discover that this particular judge, from a small town in the Northeast — come on, it's your cue to jump down my throat and call me a bigot — is not a WhatsApp user, and is actually "opposed" to technology, oops, this was actually the judge who *liberated* WhatsApp... after 24 hours of blockage. At any rate.

There's no disputing the fact that the technological revolution has changed our lives profoundly, in terms of the way we communicate. In the 1960's, the famous "revolutionary years," it was actually necessary to go to a demonstration *in person* in order to shout a couple of slogans against the status quo. What a drag! As you can imagine, there was no such concept as "virtual" presence back then, so I'll risk saying that, in fact, *this* is the significant unnamed change behind this "very unique" electoral season: furious networking. Including "The Donald's" controversial tweeting.

Understandably, this is not happening only in the U.S. In Brazil, for example, social networks have played a crucial role in the present political crisis, although the ultimate culprit in the current impeachment process was in fact... a wiretapped phone call, as in the good old days. Still, what amazes me is how these social networks have allowed us a fresh look, not only into people's opinions, but into their very souls, or consciousness. *Et voilà*, we could finally understand (at least I could) the dirty ideological game that has kept us hostages for such a long time, without exposing itself clearly until recently.

In Brazil today, there's no doubt as to how the so-called left has turned itself into a corruption scheme in order to actually rob the people, with obvious detrimental consequences for the poor and the destitute, despite the P.T. Party's proselytism to the contrary. To lighten the effect of these affirmations, let me share with you a bit of the highly efficient Brazilian humor, which is strong enough to defy the oppressive weight of the current situation: "This government has taken billions out of poverty. And deposited them in secret offshore accounts" (I hope this works properly in English, since there's nothing worse than having to explain a joke, right? Culture clash at its best).

Alright. Although I now write in English, to a certain extent I still *think* in my native language.

Nevertheless, the left won't let go easily. They are so convinced that in fact they are the righteous ones — in Portuguese, "*donos da verdade*," that is, "owners of the truth" — to the point of describing themselves instead as "owners of the good." Or so believes a friend of mine, an enthusiastic Bernie supporter who, in response to my recent (and depressive) "coming out of the conservative closet," has defined "liberal" as "a political theory founded on the *natural goodness of humans* and the autonomy of the individual, and favoring civil and political liberties" [emphasis mine].

I wonder where he got that from, because, in all honesty, I refused to google it, as I'm so tired of confronting myself with such absurdities. Let's face it: Rousseau himself (*The Social Contract*, 1762) already knew there was no such thing as "human goodness," a natural trait that "becomes corrupted by the pernicious influence of human society and institutions." Which, I suppose, must include all of our (failed) ideologies.

Curiously enough, as I was researching an efficient American idiom to describe this "owners of the good" concept, I came across a dog food commercial with the following slogan: "Feed the good." Meaning, of course, that we can, indeed, emphasize the good-natured side of our personalities under very special circumstances — which would include a stray dog about to be run over by a car, as shown in the ad, but certainly not any kind of radical political discussion. This does not entitle the leftists (oops, "liberals") — or the rightists, for that matter — to declare themselves the ultimate do-gooders, even if they firmly believe they are, which should be defined as "delusion."

At any rate, now that we know Donald Trump will indeed be the next Republican nominee, I will risk a step further into other people's hatred — once a bigot, always a bigot — and tell you what I believe is behind this "movement," which important newspapers describe as constituted mostly by white men, undereducated blue-collar workers, and misogynists, that is, men who hate women. It is a "popular revolution" of sorts, a reaction to a very typical human attribute that makes us ruin every good thing we touch, pardon my pessimism, which encourages us to go far enough in every progressive direction to eventually jeopardize its gains, without exception.

The civilization pendulum has swung, and has now reached its apex; we are all excruciatingly tired of this extreme way of thinking (and acting out!), which has found its insidious way into our daily lives, to the point of making them utterly unbearable. Its practitioners carry no interest in the common good; they only care about their own self-fulfilling goals, usually at everybody else's expense, no matter the cost. This must stop at some point. And I'm reasonably sure you know what I'm talking about.

I sincerely hope we're approaching the moment when we'll finally bid adieu to these Last Day owners of human truth, and human good. In Brazil, I know we are. Don't let the door hit you on your way out.

Narratives

A few years ago, a good friend of mine, who besides being a writer worked in advertising, was hired as a PR consultant for a P.T. candidate running for mayor in a small town in southeastern Brazil.

After a month "immersed" in the campaign, shocked by the level of corruption that she had the opportunity to witness, she told me she intended to write a book on the subject.

I encouraged her. The P.T. Party was still very popular, and although we expected the party to fall short in that particular election season (for mayors and city councils), this did not happen: Despite the fact that there were already rampant rumors of bribery and bad administration, the party came out quite successful.

My friend waited, deciding to delay her project, which, as a matter of fact, never saw the light of day. She finally changed her mind and also her professional focus, choosing to be involved in the construction business instead.

I wonder today how many responsible, good people have decided to keep quiet about what they saw and knew during all those years. I don't blame them. For our generation, speaking out has been traditionally a very dangerous business, since we grew up during the military dictatorship, the infamous "Years of Lead" (meaning "bullet material," not leadership). Although, of course, Brazil at this moment enjoys a mature democracy and complete freedom of the press, or so we prefer to believe. On the other hand, every moderately educated person knows "all that is necessary for the triumph of evil is that good men do nothing," sorry, folks.

Still, what can we do. People are free to choose.

Today, as I write, Brazil is undergoing what will probably be Dilma Roussef's last hurrah. After comings and goings and a lot of drama, resembling a typical soap opera tinted with reality show colors, the Senate will vote in favor of the impeachment process, and the president will step down for the next 180 days, probably forever. We will be free of her alleged good intentions and despicable results, which ended up almost destroying the country. Not to mention the constant imposition of leftist views, according to which P.T. supporters are the owners of the truth and of "human goodness." Imagine that.

Owners of incompetence and dishonesty, I would say. And the Law will prove this in the end. We are lucky, actually, to get rid of them while there still is some country left to recover.

In contradiction to normal logic, since ours is no more than a meaningless third-world country, I would risk affirming that Brazil today should be taken as a road map for the "leftist problem." Alright, I assume you don't know what the "leftist problem" is, or even that there is one; but if one stops to rationally analyze what is happening in the current U.S. election season, and also in the last months of the Obama administration, it will be quite clear what I'm talking about.

This week, a shocking article published in *The New York Times* candidly told the public how the American people have been manipulated into believing facts that are just plain lies. Let's face it, we have all, in one way or another, suspected this was going on, but at that level? If it wasn't so obvious, I would refuse to believe such a thing could happen in America, of all places; but there it was, in detail, including the construction of a "narrative" that would ultimately convince us of the fairness of the Iran Deal. Journalists were treated scornfully, like high school idiots. What about the common folk? Those who (rather gullibly, I should say) trust their institutions, the highly cherished ideas of their forefathers?

As a (deluded) foreigner, I confess to be baffled. And that's not all. Facebook has been accused this week of manipulating the news, favoring liberals over conservatives — following the "boss's" preferences, which would include his "dislike" of Donald Trump. Okay. Everybody is entitled to their own opinion, but not to the "manipulation of opinion," right? And this cannot, should not, exclude either Facebook staff or any Facebook users, or am I totally losing it?

Freedom of the press and love of the truth are not the only American values that have been challenged lately. I don't mean to be "square" or prejudiced, but what started as a "colorful" civil gay rights movement is now degenerating into a generalized state of abuse and depravity that would put Pasolini's Sodom to shame. I apologize for my sharp terms, but I'm so sick of it! The worst part is that it's only a symptom of where our society is heading, unfortunately.

Children are encouraged to doubt their own gender in a way previously unheard of. Morals and the traditional family are now despised as retrograde, in a world where right and wrong are no longer "absolutes," but highly debatable. "Education" has been turned into a battlefield, where dedicated ideologues play to win. And their ultimate prize is the "truth of the future," which is less and less disputed because a plurality of thought has been carefully put aside, on college campuses that have, as a norm, shunned "conservative" voices.

I loathe conspiracy theories, but it seems pretty clear that a strong "leftist agenda" is being imposed upon us, leaving little room for reaction. Thoughts and truths are being ground up in many different places, not just the political arena. I read in an article this week, for example, that Freud said "it is impossible to overlook the extent to which civilization is built upon a renunciation of instinct." To my dismay, this was quoted by an author I really appreciate, but as he targeted Donald Trump's praise of his own "gut instincts," he failed to inform us readers that actually Freud was not talking about politics, but about sex or sexual impulses — to be exact, about a "death drive" [*Todestrieb*] vs. an impulse to life [*Lebenstrieb*], described as Eros.

Freud never said anything about denying the "gut instinct" in humans as an "ability to make decisions." Come on. And even if he did, he would by now have been declared wrong, as science today recognizes the importance of intuition in our decision-making process.

And so it goes.

We all know that in ancient times History was usually rewritten by those who came out victorious in life and death wars. But nothing can be compared to today's manipulation of thought itself, a situation where, beyond a much-cherished "democracy of information," certain ideas are deemed more "moral" than others, and, in consequence, people who utter them are considered "better" than others. Who are we at war with, after all? Moreover, will we be better off if one of these "sides" is eliminated from our daily lives?

I suppose not.

More recently, the wildfires that are (still) burning in Canada were attributed to "global warming," blatantly blaming the "dirty" oil industry in the region. Therefore, I read on a Canadian friend's Facebook wall, people who have lost everything and were forced out of their homes are being accused of attracting disgrace on themselves. Come on. This sounds exactly like that despicable practice of "blaming the cancer patient for his disease," which was widely popular at the height of the "New Age" movement. Utterly unfair, to say the least.

These "narrative blowers" are so careless they despise History, and shamelessly manipulate data. Speaking of natural disasters, take, for instance, the dust storm in 1934, specifically the one on May 11, the very day when I'm writing this chronicle, 82 years later. According to historical records, "a massive storm sent millions of tons of topsoil flying from across the parched Great Plains region of the United States as far east as New York, Boston and Atlanta." Was the severe drought that caused it also due to human activity?

Alright. As a writer, I'm entitled to "create narratives," and to juggle its elements at will. That's basically what I do, and I definitely try to manipulate people's beliefs by putting together different facts that occurred at different times in a given piece of writing, in order to create drama, or at least an organized story we can more easily deal with.

But I make a point of describing my writing methods, with special emphasis on the fact that a certain degree of exaggeration is a vital part of my trade, or my style. I also insist that everything I write is no more than my own opinion, the way I see and analyze things, which, by the way, I do not impose on anybody but myself.

The people currently in charge of our "daily narratives," on the other hand, may be not so innocent and well-intentioned. Beware. They are coming for you.

THE OLYMPICS' GAME

My nephew, a 27-year-old accomplished engineer who studied in France and has been living in Germany for a few years, is coming home in August for the Rio Olympics. He filed an application to be a volunteer, was accepted, and will work as a driver: A high level professional with international experience will drive some fortunate athletes around a city that counts among the most beautiful in the world.

Like him, thousands of young Brazilians have volunteered, a long-cherished dream they started to pursue when the country was elected to host the Olympic Games, back in 2009.

It was an exciting time in Brazil. The P.T. Party has been in office since 2002, riding a wave of economic stability, and our president, Luis Inacio Lula da Silva, was kind of an icon, a simple working-class man, who, after a lifetime of struggle, has reached the highest position in Brazil — an indisputable hero of the left, recognized all over the world. Obama loved him, called him "my man." An outstanding victory for a third-world country that had been under the weight of rampant inflation not so long ago.

We have also won the right to host the World Cup, which took place in 2014 and was quite successful, despite many rumors and a political crisis that was already taking its toll.

Since then, the political crisis has escalated, reaching its apex last Thursday, when the Brazilian Senate impeached president Dilma Roussef, who was in her second term after being appointed by Lula as his successor in 2010. The choice was disastrous. Incapable of governing, after being reelected in 2014 under serious suspicions of illegal funding to her campaign, Dilma has been practically absent from the public scene for months, except for her controversial and rather senseless speeches, which turned her into a national mockery target, something the international press might perhaps ignore. Lula, on his part, has been facing serious accusations of misrepresentation, hiding of assets, and traffic of influence.

It is interesting to remember that the whole solution to the 1990s inflation came after another president was impeached in 1992, for the first time in Brazilian history. Impeachment, the pundits say, is an instrument to guarantee democracy in a Republic, when a prime minister is not in office. Without this tool, they affirm, democracy could easily degenerate into a dictatorship.

On a personal note, I've been through a number of economic crises in Brazil, and I was hit hard. Back in the 1980s, I was a successful furniture designer, struggling against 10 percent inflation. Per week. In 1990, shortly after Fernando Collor — the president who was later impeached — took office, I was involved in curating a big cultural center in Rio de Janeiro, which relied exclusively on government funding, and all the cultural programs were canceled overnight.

I also "rode the wave" of stability and progress that followed the successful "Real Plan" — which instituted the *real*, a stable currency that finally solved our problems. Albeit temporarily, since today Brazil is facing a deep recession. This time, due mainly to corruption and bad administration: Brazil does not make your life easy. So this new moment found me willing to work as a writer and an editor. I was an e-book pioneer, the first Brazilian publisher to publish an e-book in Portuguese on Amazon, long before other publishers or other online bookstores decided to risk the new market, long before Amazon decided to open an online store in Brazil. With a little help from yours truly, I like to think.

That's where the present crisis caught me. I had a booming business, entirely operated through the Internet; a catalog with more than 200 titles; and a beautiful house my American husband and I designed and built in an Atlantic Forest paradise outside of Rio. I was deeply disturbed. Not even the World Cup could cheer me up. All I could think about was selling our house for a profit and moving to the United States. I could not imagine having to start it all over again, due once again to government incompetence and dishonesty.

Now that president Dilma has been impeached, the international media has decided to accept her personal version of the facts, according to which she was the victim of a "coup." Yes, there may not be a direct accusation of corruption against her, nor direct proof of any crime. But, curiously enough, over the years Mrs. Roussef was in positions of power that coincided in time and place to crimes that were committed, as, for example, back in 2007, when the corruption scheme in Petrobras started to escalate through the Pasadena scandal. Mrs. Roussef, although affirming there was nothing against her "unblemished reputation," was the head of the Petrobras council and supposed to give her approval to any major enterprise the company decided to invest in.

At any rate, it is not my intention in this article to list a myriad of reasons why Brazil was right to impeach her, or to emphasize that everything was done 100% according to the rules and complying with democracy, respecting our institutions, and the separation of powers. Not to mention the whole process reflected the will of a vast majority of the people, many of those had actually voted for her in 2014.

I have to confess I wasn't surprised when I read this week a discussion in *The New York Times* suggesting Brazil should postpone or even cancel the upcoming Olympics. For reasons I fail to understand, a denigrating campaign was launched a few months ago by our own government, during the Zika virus crisis. Which, by the way, was mainly caused by governmental incompetence in controlling the mosquitoes' proliferation through simple, but effective measures, like we have done ever since we first heard of dengue fever, which is transmitted by the same mosquito. Immediately there was an uproar in favor of canceling the games, ignoring the fact the during the winter (in the Southern Hemisphere, winter equals our summer) the mosquitoes' population is normally diminished, and thus, contamination becomes highly unlikely.

Brazil has been accused of being good at "covering up the damage and showing its artificial face." This is not entirely true. Although our Olympic bid has been quite ambitious, work has been underway, even in the midst of difficult and troubled times. The crisis persists, but we are optimistic. We are already on the other side of one of the biggest challenges the country has faced in my lifetime, and there is plenty of disposition to show our brightest side. A fair amount of problems still lay ahead, but at least we no longer have the sensation that the (pity) party in office is doing whatever it can to keep their power intact, no matter the cost, backed up by a strong corruption scheme. Which, by the way, is being taken proper care of by the Federal Police.

Today, Brazil and the Brazilian people should be able to count on international support and all possible help to make these Olympic Games succeed. Many young, accomplished people, like my nephew, are ready to go. Rio is a beautiful city and it's getting ready for the event, our best and fastest bet to uplift our national spirit, so badly damaged in recent times. A media campaign against this important project would hurt us right now beyond any measure.

The truth is, we Brazilians are very proud of ourselves and of what we have accomplished in order to win our country back, with its democratic structures intact. Come share this feeling with us in August.

∗∗∗

Update 2017: Between the writing of this chronicle and the publishing of this book, unfortunately, there has been accusations — and proof — that Lula's corrupt practices included influencing the results that elected Rio as the host of the 2016 Olympics. The games, though, were a success.

THE FRAMING PROBLEM

It is a quiet, tranquil Wednesday morning in Greenville, and I can hardly believe my eyes and brain as I go on reading an article about "misery in America" — "an America riddled with anxieties" is the exact quote.

"Alan," I asked my husband. "Why the heck is America so miserable right now? I don't get it."

He delays his response while writing a soothing email to another promising builder, with whom we had been working almost full-time for over a month. We talked, exchanged exciting ideas on our house project — which, for some mysterious reason, is still "in progress" after almost two years. In the beginning, I was so carried away I almost considered one builder as a friend when he took us on a short road trip to show us houses he had built in the past — beautiful, nicely designed to the last detail, almost the "Architectural Digest type" we longed for. That is, if we could "afford" it.

Alan has been telling me all this time the accurate price for the kind of house we want to build — good design, clean, no rococo frills as I must have already mentioned, big glass panels and simple, but quality finishes.

We're "Bauhaus people," after all. According to him, people are deluded, stuck on a price that has actually gone down since the house bubble back in 2008, something like that. (Pardon my vagueness; I wasn't in this country back then and therefore cannot fully comprehend what happened.)

And lo and behold, after so much "courting" the handsome builder — I've concealed so far the fact that he was handsome — there came the feared estimate, around… twice as much the expected amount per square foot.

As a skilled framer — meaning, a person who "fits wooden pieces together to support a structure," also the building process of our choice — this one has tried to "frame" us alright, like others before him. But having advanced quite a bit in this construction business, we're not gullible victims anymore, so it took us only a few minutes to discover he had nearly doubled the quotes he had received for subcontracted services. *Et voilà*, we extended his "exaggeration" to the rest of the items in order to promptly reject the whole thing, to my utmost disappointment. I was depressed for a week.

I've long known as a fact, from our previous experience in Brazil — where, by the way, we had built a wonderful home, all glass and concrete on top of a mountain in the midst of the Atlantic Forest — that "all contractors are crooks," sorry for the generalization, folks. Another guy we consulted went as far as to generously offer that we "give him the lot and the house" so he could "get a loan in our place." He would then transfer the property back to us in a couple of years, as soon as we had enough credit, which I had never said we didn't. Bold. He reminded me of the desperate people I once saw in a movie who paid a hit-man to kill them in order to free themselves and their families from unpayable debt. That was not our case, fortunately.

As I've written a lot about politics lately — mostly *American* politics, a subject that doesn't quite interest most of my readership, which is still in Brazil — a few friends have asked me to describe my daily experience as an immigrant in the U.S. Something, I should add, they would not really enjoy, since I've changed my views so radically since I moved here, to the point of supporting you-know-who for President of the United States.

"Thirty-two percent of millennials are still living with their parents," Alan says, as he watches TV on the other side of the room.

He goes on to explain that the real unemployment rate is around 10 percent, maybe 15, that the statistics only count people who are still actively looking for work, leaving out those who have already given up or found another temporary solution. He argues that this administration has invested heavily in public institutions and social spending, instead of encouraging entrepreneurship to make the economy grow — kind of a "socialist" agenda. "And that's why so many people are supporting Trump," he summed up.

It is quite difficult for the average Brazilian to grasp the *real* United States. What they know does not come from first-hand experience, but through the biased interpretations of a few journalists, who, perhaps, have themselves interpreted somebody else's belief, often through "failed translations." And so the word goes. It makes a world of difference. We're being "framed," my friends, on a daily basis.

In Psychology, what they call "framing" is "the process of defining the context or issues that surround a problem or event in a way that serves to influence how the context or issues are seen and evaluated." Therefore, as I was dealing with the (difficult) house-framing problem, I came across — in the book I'm currently editing — a clear description of how the gender issue has actually been engendered in our contemporary psyches for much longer than you could ever imagine.

I was deeply discouraged. A highly biased belief concerning the "unfairness" of an "oversimplified" bilateral division of the human race into man and woman has been taught in universities as an established truth, already written in stone for a generation or so and published as valued textbooks. It's not something that has just come up through some slightly absurd "bathroom issue" in North Carolina, as it might have seemed at some point, at least for the most ignorant among us, in which I include myself.

Based on the obvious injustice in which a paternalist society has framed women for most of human history, and also on the undoubted success of the feminist movement in the 1960s, scholars are trying (successfully) to impose upon us a highly problematic frame of mind which highlights the idea that the traditional family is prejudiced, harmful to society. A lexicon which, through the smart crafting of new words and the careful exclusion of others, is producing pearls like "motherhood is not innate, but socially constructed," based upon the fact that "not all women want to be mothers." Diabolical logic. In Brazil, for example, there's a new "civil rights movement" engaged in legalizing "polyamory" — another word for "polygamy," with "extended benefits." And if this does not prove my point, I don't know what will.

As a typical product of my proudly revolutionary generation, in which women fought hard for the right to be equal to men, I'll tell you this: Having opted for not mothering children and focusing on other stuff instead, I see motherhood as being "socially destroyed" instead, and I'm sure we will end up regretting it. Too late for me, unfortunately.

In the name of all this diversity craze trying to engulf us today, it is almost unavoidable to conclude that women and men are not created equal at all. And no, this does not include "all the possible variations in the middle," if you know what I mean.

Therefore, it appears we've been founding our ideals on a frail, misleading trend, which goes on, and on, and on. Yes. You are being framed, my friends. Get out of this picture while you can.

I'm Regressive, So What?

Many years ago, I was having lunch with a Brazilian writer, who is today deservedly famous and praised, when she surprised me with the affirmation that she loved "funk" music, and everything related to it. For her, funk culture constituted an important and valuable means for women (especially in poor neighborhoods in Rio, where the genre is widely popular) to reaffirm their independence and energy, and why not, to pursue social equality.

I was appalled. I don't know what funk is famous for in the U.S., but in Brazil, it is associated with a style of rap which actually emphasizes to the letter — I mean, to every letter in the lyrics — what people are now calling "the culture of rape." This newly crafted slogan has spread like wildfire on social media, acquiring new and surprising meanings associated with the leftist agenda, which is struggling to prevail in the country despite the indisputable fairness of our recent impeachment process.

"But the lyrics are so violent," I argued at the time. "So detrimental to feminine values."

I could not convince her then. And I honestly doubt I will now be able to convince some of you of so many things

I feel appalled about, maybe because I frequently manage to surprise even myself with my newly acquired, and yet progressively consistent set of conservative moral ideas.

Before we proceed, let's finish up some thoughts about the funk... oops, the rape culture in Brazil. Last week, a 16-year-old girl appeared on a video posted somewhere (I did not watch it), naked and unconscious in a dirty bed while a mocking masculine voice off-screen said something equivalent to "Call my niggas over, and let her fuck the team" — the number of players in the team varying from five to thirty-three.

There's no disputing the fact that something like this constitutes a moral nightmare, albeit not a rarity in that particular environment, where lots of drugs, group sex and the local equivalent to "*gangsta* rap" are the norm. But what was unique in this case was the speed with which supporters of the impeached Brazilian president took possession of the tragedy and immediately linked it to a "retrogressive government that did not include women in outstanding positions and is planning to cancel all social benefits."

This is the way we have been living, I guess, in these times that can be best defined as "governed by social media." What was once the realm of educated analysis has been taken over by rushed and uninformed opinions that may "fly" or not, depending, not on the validity of the content, but on the number of followers an author has on Twitter or Facebook. Which certainly results in a mix-up of facts and a bastardized form of knowledge being widely accepted as truth, as fast as it "viralizes."

Now let's go back to a much more basic, established and dangerous reality I stumbled upon these last two weeks, as I was editing an academic book about the many forms of contemporary "paternities" (which is also the name of the book). Yes, you heard it right. The book is comprised of articles and panel texts from a psychology congress that took place last year, and as the title describes it, the main focus of this congress was the variety of possible family arrangements concerning childcare in a world where gender diversity appears to be the highest value.

As in all academic writing, all analyses are based upon citations from other authors, accepted truths published in the past, leading to the conclusion that the current "gender revolution" took root many years ago, coinciding perhaps with the beginning of the feminist movement.

I could not oppose "untraditional" family arrangements in principle, but I was outraged by the fact that, to make this "new" kind of freedom acceptable, these authors' main strategy was to destroy the inherent link between a mother and the care of her child in breastfeeding years. Forgive me if I repeat myself, but in this given context the mothering instinct was described as no more than a detrimental "biologism," a dangerous line of reasoning. If we allow it, it may result in a not so distant future in the abandonment of the old (and *outdated*) habit of generating children through heterosexual intercourse, a fact of nature which, if I may infer so, might leave a lot of gender revolutionaries quite upset. After all, who dared to let nature rule?

A touch of some sort of twisted "feminist consciousness" is quite clear in the widely spread usage of the "his/her" form in what simply consists of very bad writing. Women, who constitute the majority of writers in the field, are so worried about insignificant grammar details (such as the fact that plural forms in writing are usually masculine, much more so in Portuguese and Spanish) that they fail to perceive how, through their ideas and affirmations, they are not only allowing, but also encouraging the engendering of a social context in which women's innate strengths and natural power are being utterly denied in favor of "other minorities." Simply put, these minority groups are trying to take hold of unique biological traits as old as humanity itself in the name of I don't know what. They call it "freedom of gender," a concept of gender totally free from the constraints of sexual determinism.

In one of the essays in the aforementioned book, the writer quotes a quite famous author who allegedly studied the human family across the ages "through images," reaching the conclusion that the current preferred familial configuration (but not for long, these "gender activists" sincerely hope) is not defined by nature, referring to the fact that the idea of a nuclear heterosexual monogamy as the ideal environment for raising children was only "recently" imposed. As a replacement, for example, to the medieval habit of "selling children to a guild," not to mention the various forms of polygamy that rarely aimed at favoring women, maybe never. But of course! This is called "social evolution"!

The sad part is these theorists are very effective in affirming that something "is true of the *whole* based upon the fact that it is true of some *part* of the whole," a learned technique called the "fallacy of composition." In other words, this involves a situation when affirmations are taken out of their original context, which is very common in politics as well.

In the case of these brave new feminists, they are in fact being "hoisted by their own petard," and if not yet, they will be very soon. And so will all of us, if we don't react as fast as we can. Humanity is in danger, my friends, and I can't figure out how some fortunate humans among us are going to benefit from all this. Unless, of course, we give free rein to wild conspiracy theories that must include the likes of "global government," elimination of money and so on and so forth, all carefully designed to take away our individual strengths, freedom of expression and power of choice.

"Too late," utters my husband Alan, who, while I'm writing this chronicle, has been watching a scary documentary about DARPA, "America's Top-Secret Military Research Agency," which is also the subject of a new book that will be out next week. Alan goes on to tell me how science and behavioral research have gone too far to stop the trend in experiments that alter the human brain, including the use of "brain chips" in newborn babies and other frightening stuff.

To lump all these subjects together in the same pot can certainly be no more than a wild, alarming guess on my part, I admit. It is not different, however, from those psychological techniques that have been used to inveigle us, with the undisguised but unidentified support of the recently acquired indoctrinating power of social media.

On a personal level, I'm getting more and more acquainted with my new set of regressive beliefs, so what? And although I don't count myself among the famous 400 writers, indisputable owners of contemporary thought and signatories of a manifest in favor of the "preservation of ethics and freedom," among other slogans of the kind — I intended to quote directly from the petition, but for some mysterious reason, after being mentioned in an article in *The New York Times*, the link is no longer working — I can assure you that there are some brilliant minds out there whose thoughts are not so different from mine. Although, if we think about it, we might conclude that maybe "signing petitions" is not their style at all.

I will end today by sticking to meanings #one and #three for "funk" in the dictionary: (1) a strong, usually unpleasant smell; and (3) a state of depression, a bad mood, a low; to shrink in fright.

Yes, dear friends. With all that is going on, I currently find myself in a funk. And just like you, I have no option but to live with it.

Random Challenges

"It takes a village to raise a child," Hillary Clinton said this week in her "acceptance speech" as the presumptive nominee for the Democratic Party. A "historic step," some would say, the first woman to be nominated by a major party in the United States.

This may be a big step for us — if, as an immigrant, I may aspire to integrate myself into the "American people" — but, let's face it: From a global perspective, we are far behind. Even Brazil, where I grew up, has already had a female president, and we all know what happened back there. This turn of events does not alter the fact that Angela Merkel, for example, is a great leader, with all her ups and downs in the European journey towards a higher "civilized" standard. Which is not really working, not to mention the EU is now about to face a threat to its own existence, Brexit and all.

We must conclude... that there's no conclusion at all. Although it is indeed remarkable that women are now free to pursue and conquer the highest positions on the planet, this does not mean they will be more effective, or equal, or worse than a man. There is good and there is evil in every segment of the human race, and yes, I avoided the term "minority," because it makes no sense whatsoever when applied to an average 50% of humanity. Right? And this too must change.

Back to Hillary's speech, I had never heard the aforementioned popular saying before (please remember that, for all its undesired effects, I am still a foreigner in the United States, something my husband Alan still struggles to cope with in his daily criticism). Therefore, I immediately googled it, and found out one or two things. Sometimes a good "foreign look" can prove very valuable.

Although its origin is quite controversial, I learned that it comes from an African proverb, which seems to have been appropriated by Hillary, who was First Lady at the time, as a title for her 1996 book, *It Takes a Village*. It was more interesting to find a popular "fake quote" attributed to Hillary, according to which she once affirmed that "the primary role of the state is to teach, train, and raise children. Parents have a secondary role."

Did she say it? Apparently not. Did she affirm it in her '96 book? Apparently not. But it is a fact that she had included the African aphorism in her acceptance speech this week. Why? I was intrigued.

Why would we, women, advocate any kind of action that, at the end of the day, is detrimental to ourselves? To our *indispensable* role as primary caregivers in a human family?

It is also a fact that the idea of leaving the task of raising children to the "state" is a predominant socialist idea, which results in a greater control of human habits and behavior. Back in the idealist times of the kibbutz movement, to "use the village as a primary caregiver" was a widespread practice to which I was subjected as a baby, since I was born in Israel shortly after the Declaration of Independence, in a kibbutz in the Kinneret region (Galilee). And as women were supposed to be as available for work as men (I don't think anything similar to "maternity leave" existed back then), the care of children was (not voluntarily) confided to a specific woman in a specific house where all children lived together. Mothers went there a few times a day to breastfeed their child. It is also important to emphasize that, as far as I know, this practice is no longer a rule.

I admit that I have tried to attribute my shortcomings in life to these early beginnings. After all, it is common knowledge that the first three years of an infant's life are the ones that affect him (or her) the most. Although, in my case, I have "redesigned" my life so completely, and so often, it is difficult to affirm that it happened that way. I eventually traveled to Israel and tried to contact the "woman in charge," who was described as a strict lady, but also a caring one. When I asked her what kind of child I was, here is what she had to say: "You were just normal, like everyone else. When you cried, I just told you to shut up."

Okay. As I'm now 64, and this "investigative" trip took place almost 20 years ago, it is possible that I'm now reinterpreting her answer, mingling it with mixed feelings about my upbringing and what I have experienced all these years.

The fact is, I grew up with, and grew accustomed to an ingrained sensation of fear and insecurity, always struggling against the certainty that, sooner or later, I would lose a person or asset that I valued highly. To which I always reacted by trying to go too far, challenging myself too much, putting myself in sensitive situations I could and should avoid. I just couldn't, and still can't behave differently.

My mother once told me that after I arrived in Brazil, as a 15-month old, I refused to walk for a while. Later, as an adult, whenever I looked at pictures from my early childhood, I could detect a sad face and a body posture that seemed to avoid close contact. This used to disturb me so much that I ended up "ritualizing" these images, as a friend would put it. In other words, I decided to burn all my early childhood photos.

And why am I reminiscing about these disturbing feelings today?

I don't know the exact answer. Alan always says that, when he writes, "things come through him," or something like that, which I honestly find difficult to believe.

Nevertheless, these were the thoughts that came to my mind when Hillary said those words, and here is how I responded: It does not take a village, or a state, or any sort of ideology to raise a child. Outside of formal education, which is important, all it takes is simply a good couple of steady, loving parents — biological parents, whenever possible — a lot of touching and "I-love-yous," caring words backed by loving actions, no matter what the latest behavioral theory says.

It is not impossible for a child who is raised under dire circumstances to end up being a balanced adult, equipped for happiness. I've seen children who were wrongly diagnosed with ADD or ADHD or whatever, and medicated accordingly, and were still able to find their way. Okay.

On the other hand, I wonder why young people feel so lost today, so carried away by immediate violence and dubious beliefs, so negatively inclined against profound thinking and creative ways to transcend the hardships of life — I was shocked the other day to see a reader accusing the author of a philosophical essay of "living in a bubble."

How will this reflect upon their own children? Or, ultimately, what will our disposition to divert ourselves from nature show as a result? There's no way to know, except waiting to see.

I just thought I should write about it. Period. And as I was thinking about my chronicle today, I came across the viralized video of a six-year-old boy who reacted in desperation to another video he had seen at school, showing how mankind is "destroying the forests and killing all the animals." He was lucky (or not) they didn't teach what the real threat to the future is; and speaking of which, isn't it intriguing that we're so worried about preserving nature and animals, while doing what we can to exclude ourselves from it, struggling against what nature has bestowed upon each one of us? To experiment with animal bodies and administer drugs to lab animals is unanimously considered cruelty. At the same time, it is alright for humans to subject themselves (and even their children) to all kinds of crazy medical manipulations.

It is hard to comprehend. Meanwhile, I believe it is important, as a political stand, to fight for our right to be what we were born to be, to preserve a child's right to be cared by a loving family, protected from "social experiments." Which, by the way, would include the current "gender craze," although I'm surely aware that these same ideas can and will be used against me. After all, who is anybody out there to tell us what we were born to be? Or what a loving family is?

As a start, it is crucial to keep the "village" out of our personal lives as much as we can. That's what freedom is.

Remember: The present "behavioral revolution" began 50 years ago with acts of civil disobedience. It is stunning to realize that, today, we are begging the state to solve our most intimate dilemmas.

BACK TO THE FUTURE

Back in the ugly days when my mother was just entering her long battle with alzheimer's disease (no capitals, please) and telling deranged stories, newly crafted versions of her past, I was stunned by the discovery that all of them had a strong negative bias. I wondered why. Since she was reinventing her life, why wouldn't she try to improve it? She made a point of affirming that I hated her, that my brother and I hated each other; I even have a subtle memory that she deplored her marriage to my father, which I always believed had been perfect. (I prefer to leave the memory of my father as a great man untouched. May he rest in peace. May they both rest in peace.)

I was reminded of these sad stories while reflecting upon the sorry state of our contemporary society. Why, when, and how have we turned so negative, so violent? It is as if a dark cloud of thoughts is permanently hovering above us; once in a while, someone catches one of these evil thoughts and makes it real. If nothing else, only to justify our acute discontent with civilization, first depicted by Freud in 1929, the year my mother was born — the coincidence caught my attention.

I started writing this article with the intention of attacking cell phones and the Internet culture as the true weapons that threaten us, possible culprits of the violence and radicalization problem. To what purpose? I cannot say. Our lives, including my own, are so heavily based upon these technological advances that there's no way we can turn it around, or simply dismiss them. At any rate, why would we? It is human nature that is intrinsically bad. Look around and you'll figure out how we always find a way to ruin our best achievements and creations. My mother's sick mind was only a good example of this tendency. Okay, maybe I'm having a bad day.

Do you believe Islam is to blame? Do you believe (radical) Islam should be deemed an outdated, backwards, medieval culture, which should have been left in a cave in the Middle Ages, where it belongs?

I sure do. However, to my utmost surprise, I was in the car with Alan when we listened to a radio interview about how Sharia Law has been imposed on Muslim countries quite recently, in fact. "In the 1950's," we heard, "big cities in the Middle East were cosmopolitan and lively, women were dressed as women anywhere else and there was total freedom." Which included gay communities in Alexandria, for example, a fact the commentator supported by mentioning Lawrence Durrell's "Alexandria Quartet Series" (I added "Series" to make it sound "modern," although apparently the Middle East, with the obvious exception of Israel, was much more modern back then). Durrell knew what he was talking about, since during World War II, he served as press attaché to the British embassies in Cairo and Alexandria.

What happened, and how did it happen? If I did extensive research, I would probably find out, but this is not the point. The problem is, why are we always ready to give up hope and happiness? How can we get so involved in misery and let it carry us along?

An interesting point is how we tend to believe the first version of "truth" we ever hear, something I could understand more clearly once I joined Twitter... last week. Beyond being overwhelmed by the number of tweets (I can't believe you're not), we are also engulfed by a tsunami of inaccurate messages that find their way into our psyche, from where it is difficult to eradicate them. *Et voilà*, we are made to believe a whole bunch of false statements, which should never have seen the light of screen in the first place.

Please understand, I'm not implying that people *lie* on Twitter (except for a few, of course). They are just ill-informed, I guess, because there's no way anybody can put together a complex series of events five seconds after they took place. There seems to be some sort of online competition involving who tweets or retweets first, no matter how wrong the information may be (a simplistic and meaningless example is how they announced at first that 50 people were killed in the Orlando attack, when *only* 49 were *de facto* dead). "He who rushes eats raw" — ah, okay, another Brazilian saying that makes no sense in America, best translated by Babylon as "the fools rush in."

Who are the fools now?

A far less remarkable issue, but vital to me anyway, is how we (I mean you, my non-readers) fail to hear the truth when it's not said by a recognized pundit with millions of social media followers. It was far easier to spread the wrong notion that athletes and visitors would surely be contaminated by Zika at the Rio Olympics — an "official" truth for a while — than to read from yours truly that, in fact, there's no contamination in the winter, which is *now* the official truth disseminated by WHO. Who? Oops. I apologize.

Too late for too many of us. To my chagrin, the games in Rio are almost certainly ruined. Also ruined, by the way, are the aspirations of a number of athletes who have fiercely trained for four years in a row, having in Rio their last opportunity to shine. Nobody cares.

What needs to be changed is the way we react to these "fake news," ready to accept anything we hear on the Internet (I heard that it was decided last week we should no longer capitalize "internet," which makes a lot of sense, by the way). Let's face it, only fools fall for the first rushed version of anything that hasn't been thoroughly examined, and only "unthinking people" use their energy to spread around such questionable news to make us panic.

I'm no exception. I also spread "news" around. And I panic too. The point is, I'm getting so tired of having my sensitivities routinely overstretched that I can feel it coming: I'm eventually going to stop.

Where will I go from here? I have no idea, my friends. As I dwell on the internet all the time like everyone else, I wonder if the only way around this impossible (and worsening) existence is trying to control what we share. We should not promptly believe anything. We should wait patiently until the (((echoes))) soften, to the point when they practically disappear. Then we could (maybe) discuss the real issues. Like the ISIS flag on cell phones that could trigger attacks on this country, for example, as recently "disclosed" by Donald Trump. It makes perfect sense as a metaphor, just think about it.

I'm fully aware of having described two elements that have nothing in common, or maybe they do: Our inclination to make things worse, and our willingness to share what we don't really know. If it were different, maybe we would be sharing more art, beauty and love, instead of shootings and terrorist attacks. The perpetrators of these horrors would then be an exception, resting in oblivion, choking on their own obscurity and the meaninglessness of their evil intentions, never retweeted and solemnly ignored. But we've gone too far. And here they are, thriving among us and using the same propagating tools.

That's where we should declare our state of war and fight our back-to-human battles: online. For that's where the enemy lives. The truth is, with social media dynamics, we have finally accomplished the feat of erasing the mental filters Huxley describes in *The Doors of Perception* — a useful, protective brain feature we should cherish, despite our ardent desire to get rid of it.

Too much information does not serve us well. It has made us deaf and blind, overwhelmed by information we don't need and fail to process thoroughly.

Yet, of course, except for a Middle East "hopelessly" surrendered to Sharia Law, there's no going back in time, and move forward we must. How? You tell me.

And because nobody can stand being so miserable all the time, allow me to share a funny story: Remember I mentioned that Alan and I went for a drive? We wanted to visit a construction site to check a builder we are planning to hire. Alan had the map in the car, and effective as always, I helped him attentively and accurately with the instructions, step by step. After 50 minutes, we arrived at our destination... except it was a different location! There were two maps in the car, and I had picked the wrong one, believe me.

All we could do was take a deep breath, turn around, drive all the way back to Greenville and on to the other side of town. Finally, after another hour and a half, we reached the desired address.

Beware of the maps you follow, folks. I sincerely hope we will find our way, which will be far away from this maddening connected crowd, I'm sure.

Politics of Personal Profit

As revealed last week, a former competitor of Hillary's for her husband Bill's love is coming out in a bombastic manner: "Hillary Clinton once called disabled children at an Easter egg hunt 'f***ing ree-tards' and referred to Jews as 'stupid k***s' while Bill called Jesse Jackson a 'damned n****r,'" are a few of the "talking points" in her recently released book. Pardon the asterisks.

Earlier this week, because of an afternoon meeting, I went to the gym earlier than usual, so instead of the usual scattered human remains of *Bones* I was forced to watch *Supernatural*, a series I presently find silly. It was the middle of an episode, and since I don't follow the series, it was hard to tell, based solely on appearance, the good guys from the bad guys in the eternal battle between good and evil. At some point, one of the characters said: "She warned you I was evil. You should have listened. Now all hell will break loose." Literally.

As a young woman, when I practiced spirituality — to the point of calling myself a "shaman" — manufactured "power jewelry" and was inclined to the left, which I understood was the "right side," I made a pledge to myself to never tell a lie. It worked for a while, despite the need to work truly hard to supersede my basic education: My mother had always told me that "white lies" did no harm, and an aunt I considered a second mother tried the best she could to destroy my enlightened illusions by affirming that "in this world, only money matters."

This week, my aunt has finally won: I was too lazy (or simply not interested enough) to leave our apartment in order to "commune" with the Solstice Full Moon. It was just another full moon.

As I already implied, my pledge to never lie did not last very long. Eventually, I had a crucial, dreadful experience while working as an art director in an advertising agency, during some "feel good meeting" of sorts that was popular at the time. The psychologist-in-charge urged us all to say anything that bothered us concerning our colleagues, and I was the only one naïve enough to say what I truly felt.

The result was disastrous. Although popularity has never been my forte, after my ungainly confessions I was even more unpopular. My position became unsustainable, and I ended up quitting my job.

Today, although no longer bounded by sacred pledges, I feel free to say whatever I want, the way I want to say it. But I still struggle to make myself turn a blind eye to what I envision as the ultimate truth. I often prefer to be honest, which, let's face it, has not helped much. Especially considering the need to make money. Back in Brazil, where I left behind a massive political and economic crisis — I should add "moral and ethical," but it would be too overwhelming — it was quite easy to understand who was on the "right side," despite the boisterous noise made by the left — the "regressive left." There was no way a well-intentioned person could infer that the same people who were guilty of massive corruption, money laundering (not surprisingly, the Federal Police operation that is exposing their machinations is called "Carwash"), and, worse, bankrupting the country, were the "right guys." Even if they declared a political inclination to the left, a position intellectuals and pundits still praise against all odds, despite indications that their agenda is utterly failing. Everywhere.

However, once I "left home" and was all alone in the big, bad world — honestly, I didn't expect it to be so harmful — matters no longer appeared so clear. And despite feeling compelled to observe, to analyze, putting my uninformed, third-worldly opinions to work, I'm quite conscious of my frequent shortcomings, of the shock I experience when confronted with daily hypocrisy, and the surprising gut reactions I'm too embarrassed to share on Twitter. Which, of course, makes me a hypocrite too.

And that's where I stand today. It is a crucial week for "the future of the world," and there's no clear indication to who will win the Leave vs. Remain battle in Britain, since both campaigns were thrown into an ideological quagmire by the indisputably horrifying murder of MP Jo Cox, which, by the way, made every opinion contrary to her position sound monstrously wrong. Therefore, as a personal favor, I will spare you the politically incorrect inclinations that are burning inside me, threatening to make me hate myself into oblivion.

As a permanent foreigner in this big bad world, I feel like a bat, blinded in the dark with only my internal compass to guide me; and worse, on the edge of turning into a vampire. Unfortunately, this treacherous choice is not mine alone. Airbnb, for example, the "jewel of the new economy," is being harshly criticized for the way some of its members "choose who they will rent to," but no one can force an individual to receive a guest against his will. In the social camp, people are afraid of racial profiling, but the FBI could potentially have avoided the Orlando shooting had they kept an accurate profile of Omar Mateen. Bats. Vampires.

Now back to Hillary: At the end of the day, would you vote for a person who hides her bigotry to conquer the votes of the so-called morally superior? Or would you prefer someone else, who exhibits a fake prejudice in order to earn the votes of the country scum? Tough choice.

Meanwhile, as I was running on the treadmill (at a speed that exceeds my present physical limits, I must admit), I tried to create this text in my head while watching the *Supernatural* episode, and, not surprisingly, after 40 minutes of such divided attention, I failed to grasp the honorable battle's denouement.

It's just completely natural; it happens all the time in our multitasking, over-opinionated, uber-connected world with no borders, nor limits.

＊＊＊

A final note: this chronicle was already written under the title "Everybody Lies," but I found it "inspiring" that Donald Trump came up with a slogan to describe Hillary's public service in his Wednesday speech: "Politics of Personal Profit." Honestly, Brazilians can teach Americans a thing or two concerning this disastrous PPP policy.

A Fake Peace is No Peace at All

On a terrible September morning, back in 2001, I was watching TV at the gym in Rio de Janeiro, Brazil, when we heard the news that some undefined accident had happened.

"Did a plane just crash?" asked a preoccupied friend, whose husband was in the U.S. on a business trip.

Panic was instantaneous in the locker room. I rushed home, opened the door, dropped the groceries on the living room floor and told my mom: "Something weird has happened, turn on the TV."

We were able to watch it live when the second plane hit. "Oh my God. Oh my God," was all I could utter, in incredulity, before bursting into tears. The world as we knew it had come to an end.

In the hours that followed, our private lives were deeply affected. My mother's retirement money — funds originally inherited from my father — was heavily invested in a bank stock that plummeted in a matter of minutes. Our assets were gone. We didn't know what to do. There was no clear future ahead, and I don't mean only the economy. So stupid.

Today, terrorism and the economy are again entangled in the same week of panic-mongering news, okay, terrorism was not an issue, at least not until last night. Except it was: The immigration wave that brought with it simultaneous fears of terrorism and of competition over wages and jobs was the true motivation behind the Brexit movement, or so they say.

"Did the terrorist attack in Istanbul happen yesterday? Or the day before?" I asked Alan, while preparing to write this chronicle.

You must agree, my friends: It's been a challenge for an ordinary person to follow the news these days, when the world appears to have suddenly turned upside down.

I was in favor of "Leave," I must confess. I don't even know why, I just felt the need for a change. And despite the initial shock of "winning" — much like other "Brexiteers" I did not expect a favorable outcome — I now can envision my doubtful self in a much more positive, coherent light.

In my native Brazil, I've been witnessing a peculiar phenomenon, a mental divide among some members of the intelligentsia, who, as traditional leftists, could not bear the political corruption that have swept the country: Although they dared to oppose the ousted government due to a logical lack of choice, they still keep their hopes up for the failing leftist agenda when it comes to international affairs.

This is not my case. Since I moved to the U. S., I've been hit by a conservative wave that threatened to drown me in an ocean of impossibilities, concerning what's best for my future. And, I dare say, for the future of mankind.

Say what? Of course I ignore what's best for mankind, are you kidding me?

My husband, I need to admit, has been obsessing

over Hillary Clinton's (supposed) criminal past, and all I can do is cope with it: "Alan, stop sending me all these articles. I can't read them; I need to start working at some point. It's way past noon already!"

On the other hand, I'm now far beyond any pressure he might exert, ready to reach my own conclusions, researching on my own and capable of acting almost like an "adult" in the big, bad world. Which, of course, does not make me a "pundit," only an average normal person, who can "feel the mood," catch the wave and identify with what is truly happening — mostly through feeling, not knowledge.

Is it enough? Certainly not. On the other hand, analysts and specialists seem to be quite lost in this situation, frankly, stuck to their illusions of (where the) power (truly is). It is curious how, in this world where "diversity" is king (or queen?) when it comes to gender and immigration policies, people's urge to preserve their own diverse traits, which make them unique, typical inhabitants of their unique countries, is being despised and ignored. I miss the old days, when, flying to Europe on vacation, we would travel through very different cultures in a few days, a rich diversity the alleged "one-world concept" is trying to diminish, or at least control.

We are getting uniformed, standardized. How boring. *But why the double standard?* I keep asking myself. Why, in a world that emphasizes freedom, are some people less free to choose, to make decisions concerning their own private lives? Forced to comply with more regulations than they can possibly digest, or understand?

It sounds like a self-fulfilling hell. It's just too much for this simple foreign woman (ouch, prejudice), too much even for a writer who practices her craft outside of the dominant "progressive" tide — a painful position wherever the stakes are, plus the personal internal pressure of needing to be "right."

At any rate, no matter what the pundits say, the world has entered a time of change, and it's crucial to remain calm and give facts a chance, because, let's face it, our anxiety will not change a thing. Moreover, in a world where everyone is entitled to their own opinion, this "everyone" must not be limited to a percentage of the whole — those who can succeed in being louder than others. The "silent majority" will have their say, and they have already started, yes, those who have been discriminated on grounds of their despicable "bigotry," "isolationism," "keep-your-sexism." Who came up with these odd concepts and made them rule, anyway?

Every time the standards of a small group are ruling over the lives of the many, there will be trouble. Minorities need to be protected. Refugees need to be accepted. Nevertheless, what these "categories on the move" are seeking is a previously established set of privileges and a quality of life that will ultimately disappear, if the integration capacity of places and cultures they are moving into is overextended. Ultimately, they might not get what they're looking for, and also in this instance, the rule should be "moderation." Which, by the way, is what I expect as the outcome for Brexit: more moderation and fewer demands.

I have a confession to make: What truly called my attention before the British referendum was an alert I read on Twitter, in which a woman denounced a movement to adopt Sharia Law in Europe. It made me truly panic, I admit, less than 140 decisive characters that motivated my choice about what side to "support."

As to the market's panic, it has started to calm down,

much like what happened back in 2001. After the dust settled, there was a period of growth, and my mother's stocks not only recovered, but exceeded their prior value. However, the notion of a dangerous world has been on the rise since the 9/11 attacks, and something must definitely be done about it.

I'm not a believer in a borderless world. I do not wish to be invaded in my own home, and this is not a crime, just a wish, based on common sense. I'm not a believer in a strongly centered European power that supersedes individual countries as a condition for peace and prosperity. If not for other reasons, simply because it's a false premise. As recently seen, given the option to keep their private space intact, that's exactly what people will opt for. Regarding our individual boundaries and general well-being, "act local, think global" should be interpreted as "keep your physical reality safe, while talking online to everybody else." A borderless world should limit itself to a materialized "collective consciousness" symbolized by the internet — an exchange of information and knowledge that may propel overall progress — while preserving the sense of a factual, much-needed privacy.

Cameron's choice to offer a referendum to the British people was widely interpreted as a "*faux pas*," since the final result has jeopardized his own personal goals. But despite his political maneuvers, history had its own surprising plans. What I see is that the idea of peace tied to a borderless world is actually a "*faux pax*," pardon my pun. Peace must come from within. It will never be imposed in the long run, much less if it forces us into a situation born from detached theoretical minds, no matter their theoretical good intentions, distanced from the reality of the simple, overly despised common daily lives of real, overly despised common folks.

People don't like it. Period. Maybe the idea of listening to the people is not so bad, after all. After the initial shock, "mind your own business," "keep your family safe," and "the majority rules" might not sound as silly and wrong as the "leaders of the modern world" want us to believe. At the end of the day, it might work better for everyone, who knows?

Paraphrasing Queen Elizabeth, in Northern Ireland, this week: We may be quiet, but "we're still alive."

SECOND-CLASS PEOPLE

Words? Music? No: It's what's behind.
James Joyce, *Ulysses*

This week, a friend told me bluntly that, "if I wanted to influence the American voter, I should start by *knowing* the American voter [emphasis added]." He had just published a book that tried to do so, but, really, come on. I have no ambition to "influence" any American whatsoever; how could I? So far, I've been having a hard time just achieving a minimal understanding of the "American Way of Life," and would be perfectly happy if my (sometimes shocked) reaction to what happens here did at least raise a few eyebrows, or attracted some interest in what I write.

I'd originally planned to entitle this chronicle, "A Second-Class Citizen," but honestly, I have to admit that I haven't yet reached this level: I'm considerably less than a citizen in the U.S., although that may eventually change in a couple of years — that is, if I "behave" accordingly and learn American history, how many stars there are on the flag and so on, and how to speak English properly.

"History?" "English?" What am I saying? Or thinking?

Today, at least, I believe many Americans to be as puzzled as I am by the final proof that, yes, there are approximately 300 million "second-class people" living in the U.S. If the Clintons are first-class, and for them the law does not count (which, ironically, reminded me of one of Donald Trump's slogans, also allegedly a white supremacist slogan: "America First"), everybody else, except Obama and a few of his "acolytes" are actually second-class: you, me, and whomever you can think about in a heartbeat, including Donald Trump, the disgraced billionaire who once dared to dream that he had a political future.

As a sidebar, can you imagine the damage to the "Trump brand" once he's defeated as a candidate for president of the United States? Poor guy. He will be worse off than I am.

All of these thoughts came to my mind when I heard FBI Director James Comey's statement about the exhausting investigation of Hillary Clinton's emails, the exact same issue that, according to Bernie Sanders ages ago, interested no one. It turns out she's not going to be indicted, and, lo and behold, there goes the golden dream of conservatives (and maybe a few independents) concerning the 2016 U.S. presidential election.

"Don't be in such a hurry," Alan advised. "Let's wait a couple of days and see what happens." It turns out he may be somewhat right, given that Comey's statement sounds so much like a condemnation that even *The New York Times* labeled it as "a ready-made attack ad" — which Donald Trump metamorphosed efficiently into a video.

Alright, it's true: Some things are difficult to deny. The "silver lining" for Mrs. Clinton, the *Times* article adds, is "this is not a normal election year." Of course it isn't. Someone outside the usual political spectrum has dared to defy the establishment, and Mrs. Clinton, although, let's face it, he's not doing very well. Moreover, people forget everything incredibly fast. It will all depend on how much money is invested in the aforementioned attack ad, and on how fast Donald Trump is finally capable of "acting presidential," although, apparently, that won't happen anytime soon.

In a spectacularly well-orchestrated move (Overture: Loretta Lynch meets Bill Clinton in Phoenix Airport; Adagio: Hillary Clinton is questioned by the FBI on July 3rd; Minuet: James Comey reads his statement live, and Allegro con Brio, Obama and Hillary rally together in Charlotte, NC), President Obama embarked on a patriotic journey to elect Hillary and thereby assure his widely cherished "legacy," because, on her own, she wasn't doing so well either.

To watch the two Democrat luminaries together was live drama at its best. Hillary's undeniable political acumen (how else could she accomplish so much as a politician?), now reinforced by Obama's unbelievable, unprecedented charisma, provided an elated experience. He looked slightly bored while sitting on the podium behind her, as she described her wild adventures with him by her side, bravely piloting the American Political Drone (I wonder which of her many devices were used to reach her noble remote goals). But when he was called to action, POTUS immediately stepped into his role with rare perfection, calling upon the thirsty crowd: "Hil-la-ry! Hil-la-ry!"

She looked at him in adoration as he described her as the "most prepared, man or woman, ever, to run for President of the United States." He went on to tell the cheering audience how she had sat so competently by his side in the situation room, as they watched American forces finally kill bin Laden. What a remarkable moment.

Less than a couple of hours before, the very same behavior had been described by our investigator-in-chief — in his words, "Hillary's handling of very sensitive, highly classified information" — as "extremely careless." Which version should we accept as fact? As a newcomer, who admires the U.S. as a nation based on the law — a stark contrast to the country I come from — not to mention the "pursuit of happiness" and all that. I was disappointed, to say the least. That's when my hopes started to fade.

I haven't truly understood the real implications and seriousness of Hillary's carelessness until someone on Fox News (okay, "right-wing" media) described how she's now vulnerable to blackmailing and other violent actions by hackers who, let's face it, may not love our country as much as we would like them to. I wonder if the general public actually gets that.

Meanwhile, not so far away, Donald Trump was holding a rally in response to the much-awaited FBI event, which everyone, including my beloved husband, believed would present a different outcome. But somehow the Trump "magic" was now gone, sucked up by the dazzling charm of the competing political show no possible contempt could diminish. Although I could recognize some level of truth in what he was saying, it all registered as mere babbling. I even doubted if anyone in his audience was paying real attention.

My main reason for choosing Trump, I admit, is the way he tells simple truths second-class people like me can understand. That's right, as an immigrant I feel like a second-class person most of the time, no matter how life is treating me. Although, of course, it could be worse: As an illegal immigrant, I would be third-, fourth-, fifth-class, living under the constant threat of deportation. Which, by the way, is far less common than I initially thought.

In fact, my second-class thoughts — now, on top of it all, tilting toward the right — have been consistently increasing the daily malaise I hope will go away someday. Provided I prove myself right at least once, preferably in a very serious matter like guessing the next President of the United States. The pressure in the opposite direction is so strong that even when "we" win, we lose, and we keep constantly reexamining ourselves — take Brexit, for example. It takes a lot of nerve to go against the imposingly convincing apparent *good* displayed by the left. Moreover, presented with such irresistible charm.

Frankly, Donald Trump may not be the opportunity we seek to make ourselves heard, even if the global-reaching ideas behind the so-called Obama's legacy are quite frightening, and their palpable results so dangerous.

People say there is a "world movement" against politics as usual, which would include electing non-politicians to occupy crucial positions. But when confronted with highly developed political skills, the naked truth becomes a tough choice to make. Notwithstanding the fact that the truth is elusive, not "self-evident," much more so in such a complex status quo. It takes time and effort to deal with it, and we are much more inclined to go with the wave and let life take care of itself.

I'm not even mentioning another world tendency, highlighted this week on BBC News, this time favoring us women in high places — women like Angela Merkel, the potential British PM Theresa May, Hillary Clinton... but also the creepy Marine Le Pen and our very own nearly-impeached, unforgettably incompetent and destructive Dilma Roussef, who has recently brought Brazil down. Beware!

Oh my, what kind of treacherous sister am I, describing my own (stable) gender in such an unfavorable light?

Business as usual, my friends. Let's see where all this prolonged pain will finally take us. If it's any consolation, I keep reminding myself that, whatever the results of this election season, at least "there will be a few Jewish children in the White House." That's good.

Mine Eyes Have Seen the Glory

"Thank you for the opportunity to read and edit your very amusing sample, amusing even to someone who is almost wholly ignorant of the political machinations going on here right now," said the delightful message of a potential editor concerning my last week's chronicle. I've been shopping around to enlarge my company's staff by putting my own ass... oops, my own writing on the line. And I must confess, submitting my personal work to competent American professionals is a very sensitive experience for me — many would call it "fear of rejection."

As an ESL writer, I admit, I've been also looking for a way to break into the *American psycho*... oops again, I apologize: American psyche. And if you think I'm just trying to be funny, you got it exactly right. The pressure has been too much on my side.

The editor I mentioned above also got it exactly right: Although I've been working hard on being amusing in English — which, in fact, is my "natural style" in Portuguese, no hard work necessary — I'm mostly wholly ignorant of the political machinations in the U.S. Between you and me, how could it be any different? Even if I can't resist the temptation of writing about it, so much so that, after almost two years immersed in "the American experience," this ignorance turned out to be my subject matter, something I know quite intimately, to say the least.

This has been a pivotal week. I've even — "even" being the key word in today's piece — went viral on Twitter, imagine that. Viral in my own terms, of course, but can you grasp the importance, for a mere pretentious foreigner, to have her tweets liked and retweeted more than 50 times?

I should have considered that my keen observation skills wouldn't have just vanished over a few thousand miles, although I have been insistently encouraged to think of myself as someone inferior, second-class, with some kind of defective, irreparable outsider consciousness.

And it all starts at home, of course. I have to accept I'm still far from understanding this country, and I'm mostly ignorant of its history, and traditions, and linguistic subtleties. After all, English has more than a million words, not to mention its spelling is "random."

Paraphrasing President Obama in Dallas this week, to be an immigrant in the first world is most certainly a "humbling experience." And humbled I am; moreover, I feel repeatedly crushed, truly humiliated most of the time. My American husband, for instance, who is truly brilliant but not equally compassionate, makes a point of emphasizing my weaknesses, which makes me seriously angry. Daily. At him. At myself. Live with it!

All around us, these last few weeks, there has been a dangerous feeling of fear, of anger, of revolt, whether justified or not. And I have a firm belief that all this reactionary fever that infects us through social media just reflects the emptiness and neediness in our personal lives. In my case, at least, this is mostly true, or perhaps I just feel that way.

Anyway, I got a taste of it this week on Twitter: It suffices to expose yourself to a certain extent in order to touch a nerve.

I am not the exception. Keeping things in proportion, I have not killed anyone yet, my current "sore spot" being the building of our Paris Mountain house. As you may well know, besides being a writer and an editor, I'm also a trained architect — although a Brazilian one, therefore… utterly incompetent. So I get really crazy when my husband tries to convince me that "I don't know how to talk to people in America," and the more the time passes, and the construction hardly progresses, I get increasingly prone to frustration and violence in my own terms. Earlier this week, when he told me I shouldn't attend a meeting at our lot "in order to avoid bigger problems," I lost it, I admit. I yelled at him, and cried, and sobbed some more… and then threw a butter knife over the breakfast table in the direction of his forehead. And I hit him! Poor thing!

Who the hell was this disturbed woman? Where did all this physical violence come from? This could not be the highly educated, sophisticated me. I was so ashamed of myself, a possible collateral effect of all this humbleness forced upon my shattering proud self, if you know what I mean ("Come on, don't write that, you diminish your intellectual acumen by using these kind of hackneyed expressions," my internalized husband advises, sounding horrified).

Meanwhile, as I was breaking my back to make this text flow properly, we had the following conversation, as Alan consistently tried to distract me with the usual plethora of overwhelming information that always follows every little doubt I might express, despite my protesting that I need to focus: "What I'm saying is genius, what you're writing is ego!" *Quod erat demonstrandum.* What a pompous ass.

Now back to success: My 15 seconds of Twitter fame (and a few new followers) finally came after I made a harsh comment — "The hate is strong with you," someone tweeted — about the erratic behavior of President Bush at the policemen memorial last Tuesday, a funereal ceremony where dancing was not allowed, I suppose. He was trying his best to carry Laura and Michelle along, but it wasn't working. They were not exactly in a jazz funeral procession, much less in a touching Kurosawa movie about a funeral, and the imposing circumspection around #43 — aka "George W.," the eldest son of #41 — certainly confirmed that impression.

"I wonder if Bush was drunk in the memorial service in Dallas. He was dancing to 'Glory, glory, alleluia,'" I bravely tweeted, without restraining myself. *Et voilà*, my patriotic ignorance shone through these brilliant 140 characters, which backfired immediately: "@nogasklar (the *stupid, ignorant immigrant* was barely implied), it's 'The Battle Hymn of the Republic'!"

Let's face it: The daily workings of a recent permanent resident's life are an island of insignificant achievements surrounded by humiliating responses, no matter if you are in the supermarket, awkwardly talking to a contractor on a construction site, or worse, much worse, writing in English as a second language. So I humbly googled it, to reach the interesting conclusion that, not only the song in reference is also known as "Mine Eyes Have Seen the Glory," but it has also gone through a couple of versions, including a racist rambling entitled "John Brown's Song." Okay, I'd better "get off this train" right now, before I fall off the wagon (thank you for the idiom, fellow tweeter).

It was curious to see how conservative-sounding tweeters quickly reached the conclusion that I was a leftist, an enthusiastic Obama supporter with nothing nice to say about our last Republican president. Let's leave it that way for today, but nothing could be farther from the truth.

At the end of the day, I had learned a thing or two about America, the greatest. Literally. Late that same night, I watched a PBS documentary about the White House, and was truly humbled — not ironically, this time — not only by the courage and the importance of the United States, but also by its talent and indisputable capacity to *show* (or should I say "sell"?) America to the rest of the world, something that, unfortunately, we seem to be somehow losing in the so-called Obama Era.

Long live the American dream, because we all need it. Globally. And I mean it.

Legacy

I was having a real hard time listening to all these analyses stating that the Nice attacker was not a jihadist; they sounded as fake as the discovery that were fake the guns and grenades found in his truck — "Mohamed's 'ice cream' truck," already the stuff of legends: Eighty-four people dead, mowed down by a heartless wreck.

What difference does it make? With this indisputably criminal performance, the jihad has grown stronger anyway, and it goes on successfully "inspiring" the mentally deranged like never before. Everywhere. Does anybody, anywhere, have any doubt that the increasingly violent state of affairs we have been faced with for the last two years, since the establishment of the so-called caliphate in the Middle East, is the primary motivation behind all these horrific acts?

Worse still: I believe the violence in the world, jihadist or not, is about to reach critical mass, in which case a solution will become much harder to obtain. Not to mention the equally horrific assassinations of police officers in the U.S. these last two weeks, our very own most recent "trend."

I started this chronicle with the firm intention of making Precocious-Peace-Nobelist Barack Obama responsible for all the (new and not so new) evil in this world, including the increasingly divisive racial situation in the United States. But something in his statement about the killings in Baton Rouge made me change my course of reasoning, I admit. Paraphrasing the great Portuguese poet, Luis de Camoes, "a greater value hath risen."

Therefore, quoting President Obama (who, let's face it, if he was to be taken at the face value of his frequently beautiful words, would be indeed one of the greatest politicians in this world, man or woman, ever): "We don't need inflammatory rhetoric. We don't need careless accusations thrown around to score political points or advance an agenda. We need to temper our words and open our hearts. All of us."

Great. Indeed. That's all we need.

But it's not what I see around here. We are now in the midst of the 2016 Republican National Convention, and the inflammatory rhetoric directed at destroying Donald Trump is so violent, that I felt compelled to leave Twitter temporarily. Not that Twitter cares, not that there's any real care on Twitter: "White gay supremacist activist" Milo Yiannopoulos (there are so many senseless qualifiers out there that I had to put these in quotations to at least save myself from their hidden content) was just permanently barred from Twitter. You heard it: permanently. This, despite so much violence and bigotry and racism and anti-Semitism and anti-police activism and what have you, tweeted and retweeted freely every single day. Not to mention, of course, the ubiquitous anti- and never-Trumpism. I wonder if next week, when the much-awaited Democratic National Convention takes place, we will see these same radical anti-Trumpist great wits reveal themselves as the wonderful, fair, balanced, unbiased pro-Clintonians that they are. At any rate, I probably won't be there to watch.

The "campaign" has been so successful that, although in the U.S., as a Democracy, there's still a place for people who endorse the Republican candidate, the same is not true for the rest of world, in which most people reject Trump as blatantly as they had endorsed Barack Obama back in 2008. And on practically the same basis: none. It must all come down to different hairstyles, as the saying goes.

I find it curious that this overwhelming anti-Trump fury (people are calling it "character assassination") — which, by the way, now includes the Trump children, and grandchildren, and future great-grandchildren, and so on and so forth, forever after — not only occupies itself with mostly petty issues, like the "Trump family inclination to plagiarism," but also makes a point of simply denying reality.

I saw it. Nobody told me.

One could go at will to the RNC live broadcast and watch the enthusiasm, the manifest oratory capacity exhibited even by the previously-seen-as-weird Tiffany Trump, or the attractive previously-seen-as-stupid *Melania* Trump (this damn xenophobic Word corrector had just replaced *Melania* with *Melanie* without my realizing it), or the quite brilliant, previously-seen-as-spoiled Donny Jr. (who, now we know, can drive a tractor as easily as he drives his expensive sport cars) — okay, I apologize for sounding like an enthusiastic Trump Clan Fan, which I'm not. Not to mention a few other smart contenders in the political arena, like Governor Christie performing a live trial of Hillary Clinton's "misdemeanors" before throwing her to the hungry-for-words lions, oops, angry Republicans: "Lock her up! Lock her up!"

And then, by a single touch of the active remote, one could get a simultaneous reality check from the "opposition" channels, where, to the Dems' exhilarating content, the RNC was widely described as a complete disaster, fraught with errors, uneventful and stricken by sheer incompetence, provoking dismay on their own constituents, now irreparably ashamed of their own stupidity and intellectual limitations.

Come on. These are, on average, 50% of all Americans.

As a previously-childless-now-proud-mother-of-two old hag, I confess I was moved by the open-hearted, loving energy in Don Jr.'s voice, when, as a New York delegate, he gave his father the necessary votes to reach the "magic number" that so many pundits predicted for so long was "unreachable," at least for the despicable Donald Trump: "Congratulations, Dad!" He meant it. Believe me.

All and all, what I've seen so far is a family celebration, or a celebration of the family as the highest American value there is. But, of course, some "agendas" don't wish to score points in such a controversial and prejudiced contemporary field. They've spent too much time and energy advocating just the opposite, that is, the disputable validity and veracity of such outdated institutions as the traditional family, previously known as an oversimplified mother-and-father-and-children-cell. I understand. They are really afraid of losing their social conquests, which made our world so much "better and safer" for everyone — a threat they now qualify as the risk of "social regression."

Now, seriously, I have a confession to make. I'm so frightened by the present state of our society, by the loss of our personal safety and this regrettable, but consistent, sensation of generalized lack of hope concerning our future as a species, that this constitutes the real reason behind my decision to root for Trump, as I don't vote. We need change.

I'm well aware these retrograde remarks will come as a total surprise. I honestly believe very few people associate the state of violence and divisiveness with the crazy incentives in the direction of eliminating anything that remotely sounds like "tradition." And this would include, of course, the present popular trend in the direction of recovering national values, secure borders, "separation" from others. In other (their) words: "isolationism."

Let me be clear, here. Regarding some other person as different, and envision this difference as enriching, not limiting — notwithstanding the fact that I might not want a specific person inside my private space at a given time — does not make me a bigot or a terrible person. What I see as a true nightmare is a pasteurized world, in which, despite the rhetoric in favor of diversity, what has actually been sought is the homogeneity of humans: Everybody must embrace the same values and obey some theoretical "global leadership."

The issue is quite confusing, I admit. I could never declare that I admire extremist Sharia Law or, to be quite crude, the habit of "circumcising" women by the extirpation of their clitoris, which may satisfy some cultural habits around the world. This must stop. Period. But there is something blatantly wrong in the way we are trying to accomplish it, and it's simply not working.

Of course, to believe that electing Donald Trump will solve all of these problems is an obviously absurd leap of faith, and I don't expect any of that. But somehow, somewhere, no matter how subtly it is, something must be done to stop these world trends in the direction of "contemporaneity," which are clearly causing a lot of harm.

And this is my point today. In the next couple of weeks, while American politics is preparing to reach "the next level," I'm going to give myself a break. I have a highly personal, much-anticipated work of art to take care of, and I surely hope the world will allow me some tranquility to focus on it. At the end of the day, it makes no difference anyway, and a little bit of distance from the all-engulfing, 24-hour news cycle is highly advisable to any potential thinker.

After all, love and beauty must begin in the quiet of our homes. And hearts.

THE MANIPULATION OF THE MIND IN AMERICA

S uddenly, out of the blue — I mean, out of the DNC environment designed in blue — the U.S. is witnessing an
unexpected resurgence of feminism. A dear friend of mine,
who is in her late thirties, married, two children, suddenly
found herself to be a fierce feminist, a strong advocate of
feminine causes, and she's not alone. Even the most conservative women pundits (and also male ones, for that matter)
were unanimous in recognizing the historic significance of
the "breaking of the glass ceiling," as performed by Hillary
Clinton, the first woman to be nominated for President of
the United States by a major party.

My foreign eye was honestly astonished. What the
heck was that, all those "girls" in unison chanting their
triumph?

True feminism, as I recall, was underway when I was
a teenager, in the 1960s. I went to Google to remind myself
of our dearest icons: Gloria Steinem, Betty Friedan, Angela
Davis, with her impressive Afro. Man, we made history. At
that time, my 30-something friend was as young as "Zoe,"
["life," in Greek], the iconic 8-months-old advertised this

week at the DNC as "running for President," personifying the future of America. So be it.

Our main staple, beyond mandatory human rights and gender equality, was feminine simplicity, authenticity, including the "burning of bras." Afro hair was a must, and wild curls for white girls, and how beautiful it all was. I still cherish it, my curly hair, I mean. But today, as we all know, feminism includes the resurgence of costly stilettos, strong chemicals to "tame the mane" and other unaccountable clichés of sexual commercial exploitation of the feminine figure; not to mention the obvious attempt to steal our womanly rights performed by the 20-something variations in gender.

Do you think I'm being too tough? I haven't even started.

The Democratic Convention in Philly was close to perfection; elating, really. All the celebrities you can think of, icons of the present and of the not so present were present there to affirm their support to our next woman political hero. In a "day-after" interview on CNN, the DJ Jazzy Jeff explained what music could do in such a political environment: "People feel good, and this sensation is made to last." He did not mention the subliminal "enmeshed with the political message" part, but that's okay. It is a sad society when we trust the judgment of "celebrities" concerning the complexity of our real lives; it is all dumbed down to a cartoon, so regular folks can "get it." The whole thing resembled a movie so much that they even came up with an original theme song, "Stronger Together."

Get out of the theater, America!

Every detail in that Convention was carefully designed to respond to and attack particular points on Donald Trump's agenda, the "midnight America agenda," ac-

cording to Hillary Clinton. Now, what if it is really midnight, or at least three minutes to midnight, as the nuclear
clock is showing? I worry. There was a clear preoccupation
with establishing a contrast with the much more alarming Republican Convention the week before, by conveying
optimism and hope to America. But it was a difficult task.
Even the wonderful, charming Barack Obama, the most
impressive orator and political personality in modern
times, was exhibiting a forced smile and equally forcing his
"cool." Maybe he knows something that we don't; and still,
it was show time, folks.

The show must go on, and it did, at least this week at
the DNC Oh God, everything sounded so fake, including
the loving depiction Bill Clinton made of his relationship
with Hillary. Everybody knows it is not so, so why even
try?

Later, Bill tried to hold Hillary's hand, but she walked
the stage hand in hand with her brand-new partner, Tim
Kaine, who declared, in Spanish, that he and Hillary are
"compañeros de alma." Alright, he knows his Spanish and
made a point of showing it off, but I wonder if he really
knew what he was talking about. If he did, Bill was totally
entitled to be jealous if he ever got interested. "Soulmates,"
that I know of, refers to romantic involvement; to lovers,
not political partners.

At any rate, love was so overrated, I mean, so over-
used at the DNC — in an obvious counterpoint to Trump's
alleged "hate" — that gave the impression that the very concept of it now belongs to the Democrats. You might even
be sued for breaching intellectual rights if you ever incur
the unauthorized use of the word "love," from now on.

Donald Trump has threatened Latinos; therefore,
Tim Kaine spoke Spanish at the Convention (if proficiency

in any Latin language were a prerequisite to running for office, I could be President of the United States). Moreover, President Obama has lately held a lot of meetings with Mexico's Peña Nieto, and I wonder why. Maybe he's negotiating stronger penalties for Mexican drug barons behind the curtain, while advocating the opposite in public, one can never know.

Donald Trump has threatened Muslims and is planning to thoroughly vet them to avoid the risk of terrorism. Therefore, the Muslim presence was massive at the DNC to show their support, and this included Michael Jor... oops, Kareem Abdul-Jabbar. One of the most emotional moments of the Convention included the painful exploitation of a Muslim couple who lost their son in Iraq, a U.S. Marine officer "dreaming to be a military lawyer" (this, I must confess, affected me personally: My son is graduating from the Marine Corps OCS right now, intending to be a military lawyer, may God always protect him). At the apex of his speech, the poor man attacked Trump with his most dangerous secret weapon, a copy of the Constitution of the United States that he got out of his breast pocket and waved as a gun, targeting the audience. Except that, I discovered the next day, also on CNN, their unfortunate son had died in Iraq, yes, but in 2004, when there was no ISIS, no Islamist terrorism threat, not even a Trump threat, for that matter. Moreover, according to his accent, the man (and his mute wife) appeared to be immigrants from India, and Muslims from India, as we all know, tend to be peaceful and do not pose any kind of threat. It is true that after I wrote this text I discovered that the Khan family originally came from Pakistan, therefore the "peaceful" thing maybe would not work; it doesn't matter, the couple seemed peaceful anyway. Except that the exploitation continues: The "mute" mother even *wrote* an Op-Ed (I apologize for my sarcasm) to *The Washington Post* slamming Donald Trump.

Come on, people. Donald Trump is not demonizing all generations of Muslims that ever came to this country, although, I know, at some point he tried to blame Omar Mateen's Afghan father for the killings in Orlando. Donald Trump, let's face it, is quite incapable of keeping his tongue inside his mouth.

Which takes us to our next topic. Oh my God. This whole country was taken hostage on Wednesday when Trump declared, when commenting the email hacking scandal involving the DNC (Democratic National Committee, this time): "Russia, if you're listening, I hope you're able to find the 30,000 emails that are missing." By God, he was being ironic! How could he not? As someone reminded us, he was "inviting" the Russians to hack into a server that no longer exists and find emails that were erased three years ago!

All hell broke loose. Trump was accused of being a traitor, a Russian agent and a friend of Putin's. Suddenly, out of nowhere, we were back to the glorious, hysterical days of the Cold War, and the country was transformed instantaneously into a live version of "Saturday Night Live" — an embarrassing joke on all of us most people failed to recognize. Nobody mentioned the real problem, that is, the explosive content of the DNC hacked emails, which proved the ex-chair Deborah Wasserman Schultz (who was forced to step down on the eve of the Convention) to be guilty of manipulating results in disfavor of Bernie Sanders.

People seem to fail to understand why these comparisons between Hillary's and Trump's accomplishments in public service don't make any sense. Donald Trump was never in public service. Until a year ago, he was in the private sector, a regular American entrepreneur. Which, by the way, would explain why the ties and clothes and shoes that carry his brand are not "Made in USA": He would simply go to where the manufacturing is currently more advantageous, that is, China — just like Apple and all the other big companies. Patriotism does not include business profit, it never did. And for the sake of electoral logic, better no public record than a blatantly bad one, like Hillary's.

A woman I talked to this week in Walgreens criticized Trump because she "distrusts any person who feels compelled to write their name on everything they own"... "Like Trump does," she added, while equating a work colleague of hers — who does that on notebooks, tags and Tupperware in the office's refrigerator — to a businessman who has developed a brand, like Versace and Chanel, for example. And so it goes.

An emotional Joe Biden made his convincing contribution by lamenting that someone, anyone, with a "compassionate, typical American upbringing" could get any satisfaction from saying, "You're fired!" By God, people. Trump said that on a television show! Don't you see that? He was not firing a *real* employee, who would lose his benefits and jeopardize the security of his family, but some reality show participant, whose primary goal was to resist being fired until the end of the season!

It was not real life, *capisce*?

On the last day of the DNC Convention, responding to the "offensively stupid" Trump's comments concerning the absence of American flags on the floor, thousands of "USA" signs appeared and the crowd was cheering accordingly: "USA! USA!" But... this was not proof that Democrats are prone to patriotism. On the contrary, it was proof that "only Trump" truly gets it. Even if the "USA fever" that had taken over the RNC last week was a reminder of Reaganism.

The last attempt to destroy Trump in Philly was Hillary's comment about Trump's infamous remark, "I alone can fix it." She reacted in triumph, "in America we do not fix things alone... we fix them together!" A roaring, exhilarated echo ran through the audience: "Together!" But, folks, even a pretentious foreigner like me knows that they were intentionally misinterpreting his words: "I alone can fix it" means "I'm the only one who can fix it," not "I'm going to fix it alone." @realDonaldTrump himself has said it in his acceptance speech: "We are a team."

And since we're down to Twitter identity (by the way, Hillary Clinton has declared: "A man you can bait with a tweet is not a man we can trust with nuclear weapons"), let's check the latest numbers: Donald Trump has 10.5 million followers, while Hillary has *only* 7.89. Which means, if Twitter counted, he would trump her by almost three million, folks. The people hath spoken.

Let's face it: This whole manipulation-of-the-mind business should not come as a surprise to anyone. After all, someone has already declared that "If we want your opinion we will give it to you." And I'm not alone in perceiving it either: An interesting article published this week depicts the psychological techniques used at the Conventions — both of them, for that matter, although much more money has been invested in the Democratic one — in order to, literally, manipulate our minds; and this would include the blue background in front of which important speakers were carefully positioned.

I'm sorry, but I am profoundly aggravated by all of this. So much so that I was forced to leave my "personal project break" in order to come here and share these humble considerations with you.

Pay attention, America. It is our own lives that are at stake, not "someone else's."

A CONCRETE FOUNDATION

While I was away, compiling, re-translating, and re-writing my novel *No Degrees of Separation* (yes, all of those, in interchangeable order), several subordinates of a powerful media mogul accused him of sexual harassment, and he stepped down as a result. He was 76 years old. There were also a few other TV stories about rape, especially as a crime widely disseminated on our college campuses.

What do you think is going on?

During the first week of my self-imposed break, still feeling the effects of not writing my weekly chronicles, I began to draft an article entitled, "My Personal Experience with Rape," or something like that.

Rape is a crime: period.

However, I was never raped.

Nonetheless, I surely had some unpleasant experiences with sex. I once awoke with a stranger in my bed after a night out wasted, went home with another because I felt lonely on Christmas Eve — I'm Jewish, and we never celebrated Christmas at home — and tried to reap some pleasure from having sex with the brother of a man in whom I was interested romantically (unsuccessfully).

My worst experience ever was with a man with whom I was working when I was in my thirties, and single, after my first divorce. He was a sub-celebrity, as they say these days (they actually call it "Z-list;" I just read it in *The New York Times*), a theater and media personality of sorts. I was creating the graphic design project for a play he was producing and directing. I have made a point of forgetting his name; at any rate, he was much older than I was, and it's likely that he is dead and buried by now. This man came to my apartment one day to discuss a few details of his project, and when I told him I was feeling tired, he offered me a relaxing massage. I accepted. The next thing I felt was his wandering, inconvenient, unsolicited finger entering my vagina and rubbing my clitoris. Disgusting! I told him to stop and leave immediately. I felt dirty for a week, and refused to work for him ever again.

During my first fifty-three years of free love, sex, and rock'n'roll, I had never had an orgasm with a man, but this is not news to those of you who have read some of what I have written.

I wonder what is wrong with our society, and with our young women, after all these years of sexual revolution and the fierce fight for women's rights. If I were prompted to give advice, I would tell these girls: "Don't drink and party on the same night; or at least, don't drink yourselves to the point of losing self-control and not knowing what you're doing."

However, to my readership's chagrin, I would go further: Don't mistake unsolicited sex or sexual advances for rape, as these are fundamentally different acts.

We hear, read, and watch such a plethora of sexual messages today that we have lost a proper notion of what sex actually is, and how important it is. So let me repeat it: Sex is the source of life; nothing more, nothing less.

Thus, I spent the last five weeks, which began shortly

after the Democratic National Convention, away from the political scene in the U.S. (and in Brazil as well, for that matter, where, after a long and painful democratic process, Dilma Roussef was finally ousted from office), dealing with a more profound and much more exciting subject: sex and love in the technological era, as well as with my personal journey from "never coming" to "coming whenever I was prompted to do it," from "never being loved as I wanted," to "being loved in return as much as I wanted."

It was a big deal, and it left me wondering about what is important in life.

I now have the answer: it is love.

Before I could summon the necessary energy to deal with my ten-year dream of publishing my novel in English — which, by the way, is the language in which the original material was written — I was deeply involved in the "political machinations in the U.S.," as a friend described it. To transform the text into literature, I must add, I was forced initially to write the novel in my native Portuguese, facing my shyness and difficulties with written sex, and to improve my writing skills in English as well. However, I always suspected that, although politics is important, the reason why I was so involved in it and so worried about it, was that, well, in these first two years on American soil I was actually living a temporary, improvised life. I also was quite frustrated and unhappy with a couple of aspects over which I did not seem to have sufficient control.

It comes as a delightful coincidence that, as I'm completing my novel's journey, Alan and I have also been able to deal with the (abundant) initial hardships of building a house on top of Paris Mountain — "taming the mountain," as I like to call it — and are about to pour concrete into our foundations, believe it or not. Sometimes I do, but sometimes I don't. It all feels like a weird dream in which I watch myself living a life that does not seem to be my own, and yet it is. This makes me face it with a certain degree of indifference that might as well be protective, and somewhat positive, as it prevents me from becoming overwhelmed by anxiety. I am inclined at present to stop resisting the old and previously despised temptation to see a sign of something in everything else — a Shamanic tic I developed in the past —, as I realize that, in fact, love and sex are the pillars and concrete foundations of human life on earth.

Curiously, my personal memoir of written love and sex was a testimony of the very first online dating adventures, when the capacity to express oneself in writing was crucial to developing deep ties with someone who lived on the other side of the planet, a practice which incredibly enhanced the chances of finding love. Yet, sex turned explicit, the meagerness of 140 characters and the ubiquity of cell phones capable of filming and photographing everything and everybody, everywhere, doing anything, transformed this elating erotic exercise into mere, lamentable sexting, pure poverty of spirit. This week, for example, this tendency culminated in the final demise of a sub-celebrity made ex-congressman and about to be an ex-husband, all because of his vulgarity on the cell phone keyboard.

Here is what I have learned: Whatever comes up in our lives and in the lives of those around us, we must never lose sight of what truly matters in life. These things last, enlighten us, and make us feel like the precious animals we are — superior, yes, for we are endowed with a brain that thinks (and learns from experience) and an astounding body capable of incredible feats.

Believe me, we should never, ever accept anything less than that.

The Perennial Myth of the Evil
Mother-in-Law

L et's face it: Writing confessional literature is a high-
risk job, and as such, should be compensated properly.
Moreover, to avoid the potential destruction of marriages,
families, and long-standing friendships, the degree of truth
and transparency should always be balanced with homeo-
pathic doses of pseudonyms, pen names, and similar *pseu-
dos*, together with character displacement, notwithstanding
the fact that, in these particular cases, the resulting literature can no longer be considered "confessional."

That said, the other day I ran into a colleague who was
highly distraught, in a truly sorry state. I could not exactly
"empathize" with her, because, as my shrink friend well remembered the other day, not being a mother I could never
really be a mother-in-law, not in a million years. The closest
I could get to that dangerous situation would be if I *elected* to
develop a friendship with my husband's children and their
potential spouses, which, of course, I would enjoy. That is,
if I had the slightest inclination to form and maintain nice,
smooth relationships with people for whom I care. Nevertheless, concerning their opportunity to become intimate with

my outstanding persona, it is practically up to them, and to how much they would value the necessary effort.

Now, back to my friend: She had just had her first "inevitable" clash of opinions with her daughter-in-law (or at least that's how a few Facebook friends qualify the mother-in-law/ daughter-in-law experience), with whom, by the way, up to that crucial point, she was getting along pretty well, at least for a first-timer. The worst part was the poor woman had never had a choice, as the younger one was pretty overbearing, or so she told me. Even more painful was the fact that she seemed quite deluded, influenced by the overwhelming political propaganda exercised by the media in a typical American electoral year.

With respect to this last statement, let me tell you, I could relate very well, as you might realize. As a foreigner going through my first election cycle in this country, I confess that I feel puzzled and lost most of the time, as I already wrote in previous chronicles. And, oh, boy, there's no describing accurately enough how unique and distressing this cycle has been so far, even for more experienced American citizens who never tire of emphasizing it on TV, social media, you name it. Now I find myself so exhausted with the whole shtick that I stopped tweeting and reading tweets altogether. I still visit *The New York Times* website occasionally, but I'm very picky about what I read, as I'm not willing to upset myself unnecessarily. Therefore, I try to limit myself to the cultural sections — a book, a play, the occasional movie review — which, as you know, are considered fairly irrelevant at this moment... or is it just me?

I invited my friend for a cup of coffee, and as we were heading to the nearest Starbucks, she finally confessed her deepest fear: She would do anything in her power to guarantee the love of her (yet unconceived) grandchildren, of which, of course, there's no guarantee whatsoever, because love, as my mother taught me, has to be "conquered" and demands "an effort." That's right; I'm that traumatized. Because of my mother's deeply ingrained beliefs, which she made a point of transferring *into* me, I ended up quite incapable of just surrendering, simply allowing myself to love and be loved, and life to take its course.

The problem was, the mother- vs. daughter-in-law dispute included that the nobody-knows-when young mother-to-be forbid my friend explicitly from visiting her unborn grandchildren: A rude awakening indeed!

I could understand my friend's distress completely, and offered her my solidarity, poor thing. Of course I could not understand any of that... I could scarcely imagine what a pregnant woman goes through, and how she manages to navigate her shaken body awash with hormones.

Don't get me wrong: I always believed, like most of you, that pregnancies are periods of bliss and beauty, the supreme realization of a woman who is "born to breed," so to speak. Not that I have ever experienced anything like that first-hand, so I must accept other people's opinions... with the exception, of course, of what I can research and read, and edit, for that matter (in Portuguese, of course).

So it turned out that a couple of days before I met my friend, I was editing a text that, to my utmost surprise — and shock, I must admit — described motherhood as pure violence and torture. According to the authors of the article, who were of two different genders (among all of those variables about which we have been extensively lectured nowadays), the sensation of a human growing inside another human could only result in indescribable unpleasantness. The aforementioned waves of hormones often resulted in a state of mind akin to clinical psychosis. Then there was the terrible nuisance of having somebody else's foot jammed under your ribs, your bladder capacity diminished drastically, and the unacceptable inconvenience of being kicked from within constantly, and more, witnessing the contour of body parts appearing under your belly skin — a nightmarish description that could only be compared to those despicable B horror movies from the 1980s, prior to the development of 3D techniques and digital special effects.

I swear to God, I'm not exaggerating one b... well, maybe a little bit. But on more general terms, this was the true content of the said article, which ended up justifying the "more than natural" filicide impulse, plus hatred and vicious sexual manipulative acts directed towards the newborn infant once he's out of the womb.

It left me wondering, and I reached two conclusions. Firstly, I understood how lucky I am to have survived all these murderous impulses and body-and-mind invasive parental tendencies, together with the countless issues I've faced because of my education; and secondly, to my dismay, I could not fathom any alternative way of sustaining humanity that would spare poor potential mothers and fathers from such unavoidable suffering. Unless, of course, upcoming technological improvements — that, I learned earlier today, might include a much more effective way to obtain sexual pleasure by having intercourse with robots — will allow us, perhaps, to generate a baby through an effective cell phone app.

In all honesty, I'm grateful that I'll probably be dead when all these frightening "diversity-praising" and "liberal" analyses and predictions about the most basic survival mechanisms of the human race finally come to fruition.

As for my friend, by means of consolation, it does no harm to remind her that, after all, "the best-laid schemes of mice and men gang aft a-gley."

The History of my Tooth

When I woke up early on Thursday morning (too early; it was practically dark), I suddenly realized that it was the first day of autumn, my current favorite season (unrelated, of course, to my "autumn years"). So, I rolled over and pretended I would sleep late for a change, just as if there was nothing waiting on my long to-do list.

My agenda these days has been so overwhelming that I must admit I feel exhausted even before I wake up. This is because not only do I have an excess of projects to work on simultaneously, but also because of the increasing number of new skills I need to acquire to cope with these projects' demands. Further, my brain itself is also approaching, step by step, the aforementioned "autumn years."

Yesterday, for example, I had to reach a rapid understanding of the previously unknown concept of the "roof pitch index," which I hadn't learned in the School of Architecture back in Brazil. My favorite building style used to favor flat roofs only, no pitch at all — a serious issue I needed to overcome to become a "South-Carolinian" at heart. Now, at last, building a legitimate "Southern Craftsman Home."

Okay. Let us pretend there's no elephant in the room, that

is, the much-delayed release of my novel *No Degrees of Separation*, after working on it for 12 years… which will happen on November 15th, *exactly* 12 years after the day I started writing it online with my husband, Alan. Maybe I'll gather enough courage to write about it in a future chronicle, who knows?

Nevertheless, regardless of these remarkable achievements in my bumpy American immigrant trajectory — book and house included — the important insight of the week actually revolves around a missing tooth, and the mandatory changes we all go through.

Frankly, the disappearance of this tooth, molar #30, came as no surprise at all. I was actually born without it, and also without #19, its twin on the left side: a perfect symmetry of absence, although as a child I did have their deciduous correspondents, "K" and "T."

Mr. K, I'm inclined to believe, was the first to go, on a hot summer day in Rio. When its surrogate #19 didn't show up, we simply replaced it with a removable bridge, and that was that.

It was alright, despite the fact that I was utterly self-conscious of its presence in my mouth most of the time, and had to place the humiliating fake tooth on my nightstand every night before going to sleep. The situation became utterly unbearable a few years later, when, on a Carnival morning, while my dentist was out of town for the long holiday, I started to lose Mr. T as well.

I had been losing enough those days, including my second husband, to whom I was more attached than I'd like to admit. Back from Brasilia with a failed relationship on my back, which had started so promisingly on the internet, I decided there was already too much on my plate. Therefore, I should allow myself to move forward, adopting some extreme measures to avoid dealing with two removable bridges at once, one on each side of my jaw, both having to be removed every night of my future life.

My car had been hit recently in its parking space near the back entrance of my mother's building, so I sold it for thirty pieces of silver and invested the entire amount in a couple of dental implants, a technique that was in its infancy in my native Brazil.

The surgeries (one tooth at a time, separated by 15 days) were frightening, to say the least. I was laid down in a dentist's office all dressed in blue to simulate a classic operating room, and remained there for hours with my mouth wide open, listening to the troublesome chatter of the two professionals who were performing the procedures, and who might or might not know what they were doing. When I had barely recovered from the first, I went in for the second, much worse this time, not only because I knew what I was about to endure, but because the surgeon had decided to implant two teeth rather than one on the right side, the mandatory #30 and an unjustifiable #32.

My body did not enjoy that at all. Back home from the second procedure, I felt as if I had been run over by a truck, and the night that followed wasn't any better: I couldn't sleep and was feeling delirious, running a high fever. In the middle of the night, the rebellious #32 abutment jumped off my jaw, implant and all, and landed in the middle of my painful mouth. I took it out, placed it on my nightstand, and went to sleep, pain and fever suddenly gone. The next morning, I put implant and abutment in a Ziploc bag and walked three miles along the beach to the dentist's office, feeling greatly relieved.

"What brings you here today?" the dentist asked.

"This," I said, dramatically, defiantly placing the rejected implant next to his hand.

He still tried to convince me to undergo another nightmarish procedure, which I emphatically refused. He also declined to refund the amount I had paid in advance for the future crown, so I told him… well, something a lady should never tell anyone, and instructed my bank to cancel the checks.

Honestly, I have been reasonably fortunate with these implants over the years. With the exception of a minor nuisance with #30, which at some point needed to be fixed (by another dentist, of course), I have lived peacefully and comfortably with both of them. Until…

We were driving to Atlanta the other day to renew my Brazilian passport at the local Consulate when my tooth began to ache. *Weird*, I thought, *this is not even a tooth…* and proceeded to adopt my usual resilient attitude, convincing myself it was simply a side effect of a normal migraine. But it wasn't. When I finally gathered the courage to investigate it properly, I discovered that #30 had loosened completely, and on the eve of Labor Day — a long holiday, just for a change.

When the American dentist finally saw me the following Thursday (I was lucky enough to know one), my tooth could not be saved: The implant had broken in half, deep inside my jawbone... or maybe it had been broken from the beginning… who knows… I soon learned that it is quite rare for an implant to break in this way, not to mention "extracting and replacing a broken dental implant is a complex surgical procedure." In my case, as nothing with me is that simple, the dentist informed me that it was actually a "high-risk" procedure, as the remainder of the implant was dangerously close to a nerve.

At any rate, it would be fair to debate: What would be the purpose of dedicating an entire chronicle to such a highly uninteresting story as "the history of my tooth" since birth?

In fact, I was utterly surprised by my attitude about the missing tooth: A situation that was unbearable, practically unthinkable, 20 years ago, did not bother me at all today. After the initial shock, I was quite open to the dentist's suggestion: "I know it sounds terrible, but the best option for you would be to leave it alone, with no tooth replacement."

It is true that our self-perception changes dramatically over the years, and so do our most cherished values. Today, no matter how thoroughly I examine my open mouth, the empty space seems to be barely visible, and if I hadn't decided to write about it, it would be imperceptible, albeit unforgettable to my restless, ever-probing tongue.

On the one hand, despite the strong impulse to currently expose ourselves on social media, which we all must guard against to preserve our "personal privacy" to a reasonable degree, who the hell cares about what other people will think or say? Even the great Pina Bausch had a missing tooth, much more visible in her case. On the other hand, the world seems highly invested in forcing us to think the way they want us to think, and it's getting worse by the day. I feel appalled every day by the way the "imposing left," for example, has not only been ruling our lives, but also cluttering our real existences by shoving upon us their theoretical deliriums, insanely crafted in their globalized symposiums, allegedly designed to "save humankind."

Let's face it: Their pretentious assumptions have proven to be as fake and intrusive as my failed implant, and it took them more or less the same amount of time to come up with their concrete, detrimental results. It all looked so much better when we were young and willing… didn't it?

When we fully supported these ideas in the first place, so full of promises, so inflated with modern foolishness.

At any rate, today, like my lost fake tooth, it is time for them to go.

THE LADY IN RED

After the first (and foremost?) presidential debate between Donald Trump and Hillary Clinton, the most rejected presidential candidates in recent American history, I asked my brilliant (and authoritative) husband Alan: "*Nu*, after all these documentaries and debates, are you still in favor of Donald Trump as President of the United States?"

At first, he was quiet. Then he did his best to escape a full answer.

"Hmm… well… I *never* said I was in his favor; I only said he was going to win. He *is* going to win."

As has turned out to be the rule these days, this is not the *real* truth. The real truth — which of course could and must be warped by my increasingly defective memory, or so my enemies prefer to believe — is that Alan had chosen Donald Trump as "his candidate" from the very beginning (albeit an American citizen, Alan had never voted and never will, according to his own disposition), when there were *18 Republican candidates* to choose from, as I made a point of reminding him.

I didn't. Because I was deeply traumatized by my choice of Barack Obama in 2008, back in 2015 I decided to go for a more "conservative" option and chose "low-energy" Jeb Bush as my favorite. However, it soon became obvious that "Jeb!" was never going to fly, and when I was ultimately faced with Trump vs. Cruz, I essentially had no other option but to go with Trump.

I have been able to keep my vote ever since. To be honest, I've also kept my mind open and have been tirelessly analyzing, or trying to analyze each of Trump's steps in his bumpy road to the White House. Maybe.

Let's face it: I was practically sure that The Donald and I had nothing in common, especially because, not only have I struggled with money all my life, but I also *make it a point* — a completely senseless point, I admit, even more so in uber-capitalist America — to keep money and work 100% unbound, not even related. I don't know; maybe I've fallen victim to some oversimplified version of Christian guilt, added to a core rejection of the widespread and quite prejudiced belief that "all Jews are created financiers."

Nevertheless, I quickly overcame this first impression. I soon discovered that Donald and I shared a knack to graciously offer people their true-natured names (aka "name-calling" or, on the positive side, "nicknaming"), together with a few "buzzwords" (or better, "buzz expressions," as demanded by my stubborn ESL personality), like "believe me." In my case, Hillary's acid response, "I don't believe you" would be utterly unnecessary, as whenever I write the words "believe me" in a chronicle, you'd better not.

At any rate, today, even after the aforementioned debate, I'm still a Trumpist. Deplorably. Believe me.

Hillary had had a bad week, coughing, falling, pneumonia, and all. Poor old hag, I can hardly imagine all she has been forced to endure in this merciless presidential race — a meaningless test, at any rate. No matter what hardships people face when seeking the highest office in the land, it is still a "free sample" of days to come, in case they reach their goal not only of acting presidential, but of *de facto* being the president, day in and day out, oh my God, for at least four years. What a tremendous hassle!

At any rate, when she walked onstage that day, one could perceive at a glance that it was a winner's entrance. The red costume, although carefully hiding her arms and legs (probably and regrettably as cellulite-ridden as my own), as has become her "style," looked ravishing, defiant, screaming "self-confidence." The hair had freshly added, "sun-kissed" highlights, and certainly looked fluffy and soft, in strong contrast with other less enticing, weary looks she had exhibited recently. The makeup was also perfect, a smoothly conceived mask artfully designed to disguise her years. All of this was topped by a constant, radiant smile, to which she added the occasional shimmy that turned out to be the "trademark" of the debate. A true star.

Who could beat that? Certainly not the weird-haired, disgustingly masculine looking (and acting), rich, old Trump, who, it turned out, couldn't keep his mouth shut to avoid bragging about his "smart-businessman-ass." It was beyond the pale.

"In all fairness" — another of Trump's famous buzz phrases — with so much theater and advanced media techniques, designed specifically to make you believe whatever "they" want you to think and act upon, it comes as no surprise that not only a (tiny) majority of Americans, but also the majority of the world, have no doubt that they must opt for Hillary, without any hesitancy. They *must* know better, in such a complex and dangerous world as ours is today, right?

I, for starters, must confess that, forty days before the

election, I still don't know what is best, except that it's not Hillary. Especially after my "beloved" Obama's redemptory proof that he was *after a legacy* from day one, regardless of the effect of his beautiful words, which could or could not be transformed into facts. Mostly not, as time has shown.

A sidebar: As someone belonging to the méti-er, I cannot stop myself from pointing out that Hillary's much-appreciated campaign logo is dangerously simi-lar to that of a government agency. Moreover, this is her last-ditch effort to realize an old political prophecy: "Eight years of Bill, eight years of Hill." End of sidebar.

Especially this week, it is sad to realize the true stat-ure of politicians today, mostly liars and cheats who are utterly disdainful of their people's needs or pain. For this week in particular, an old school politician, a pillar of jus-tice and goodness (or so I sincerely hope and like to be-lieve) has left us for good: Shimon Peres, the last founding father of the State of Israel: History has turned a page.

In all honesty, I have no idea where this world is heading. Still, after the twists and turns of destiny, and the disturbing outcomes of the well-intentioned revolutionary ideas promulgated by our baby-bummers generation (I'm so sorry for my despicable pun, but in our gender-crazed days, it is almost inescapable), it is somewhat refreshing at least to maintain the *illusion* that somebody out there shares my daily, down-to-earth, *simplified* thinking. That person would be Donald Trump. Further, I surely expect him to surround himself with capable, experienced, down-to-earth, yet well-informed officials who will advocate for commonsense progress and concrete, realistic goals.

I was planning to finish these ramblings today with an intriguing affirmation I heard the other day on TV; it compared some outstanding historic American figures, such as, let's say, Harry Truman, who rebuilt a Europe devastated by WWII, or even Ronald Reagan, who helped destroy the "good communist" myth, to a Barack Obama whose most palpable legacy is the creation of "transgender bathrooms." Unfortunately, I failed to write it down at the time and could not find it later — as you all know, an unforgivable sin for any attentive chronicler who deserves the name... and for that, you must accept my sincere apologies.

Home is Where Your House Is

O uch! Have you ever lost $915,729,293 in a real estate investment?

I suppose not. Neither have I. And I honestly don't have the slightest idea of what this kind of money feels like, let's face it: Last week, I hesitated to spend a mere $498.00 to publicize the most important book I've ever written, the biggest project of my life... except for the next ones, of course. Maybe that's why I have never been a (monetary) success in business. Who knows? Maybe it's time to change, and decide to embrace the true nature of capitalism that boosts the American Way of Life, as Trump always has. Nevertheless, despite my modest income, I confess that I did what I could, with the help of an accountant, to take advantage of all possible deductions in my first tax return in the land. Was I wrong?

At any rate, I was all prepared to write about politics again today, when I realized early this morning, as I drove the winding road up to Paris Mountain to check the construction of our future house, that I have other struggles in life to worry about. Moreover, although I've already written a significant number of books (at least in my native

Portuguese), planted quite a few trees, and built a wonderful home in Brazil, building this house in South Carolina has been the greatest challenge of my entire life. I'll have to pass on the child, unfortunately. However, I've occasionally played the mother with a fair amount of pleasure — with my stepchildren, and with the couple of hundred authors whom I've published so far, who feel KBR is their family, or at least their literary family.

It's difficult to describe what came over me when I saw the house in all its height for the first time, harder still when I decided to cross (crawling, trembling, on a narrow, fragile board) the 3-foot moat that currently surrounds our private castle on the top of the world, as I could not resist the urge to enter that house for another minute. There was also the equally indescribable emotion of witnessing the project that I've been drawing for two entire years on a flat surface, acquiring volume before my very eyes — a pleasure nonpareil.

Currently, these are plans #29, in addition to the *professional* architect's ones, which were discarded because they were impossible to build, go figure. In addition, we still need to do some fine-tuning, not to mention the complex task of choosing all the finishing materials. I expect Alan and I to obsessively discuss every little detail, as he's still seeking the perfect "American quality" as he did eight years ago, only this time in the right locale.

Anyway, it already feels like a sort of miracle that this long-awaited building, which for the last 24 months seemed to be quite the impossible dream, is finally taking form.

It wasn't easy. It's been exactly two years since we arrived in this country, I as a wannabe immigrant, with the (meager, I discovered in a short period of time) assets from the sale of that other dream house we had left behind, along with our crumbling Brazilian lives.

At the time of that other construction in the midst of the Atlantic forest, I swore to God I would never, ever go through this kind of painful endeavor again. Every detail needed to be debated (and translated back and forth, because Alan never learned a word of Portuguese) seeking that aforementioned "American quality," which, of course, is nonexistent in Brazil — a country without standards, where we practice the art of improvising in every aspect of national life, including the building of a house.

I still remember Alan's desperation when he discovered that the back wall on the second floor was completely crooked, not to mention our disappointment when we faced the beautiful picture window in the dining room for the first time, when it was still divided into two shy, modest, narrow openings, soon radically transformed by knocking down a few bricks.

One night, I got up in a panic, woke Alan up and told him the bathroom door in the house was set inside the frame to open in the wrong direction; which, curiously enough, I had not realized when we were at the construction site earlier that day. Lo and behold, I was right. It was the most difficult feature to fix in the entire project. However, once we moved in, we had six exhilarating and very productive years as a result, until the situation in Brazil went truly awry — too tough to handle, to be exact.

I would be lying if I told you I hesitated for a minute before deciding to sell the house and move out of the country. The cherry on top was to find the right couple, who would cherish it and value it, and who even now keep sending us pictures to show us how well they've been caring for Alan's roses. We had left our heritage for others to enjoy, a touch of art, a white diamond on that distant mountain top outside of Rio.

As Alan used to say, "You live in a sanctuary or you own it." In fact, he said "monastery," but our house in Tranquility Valley was more of a sanctuary, with the imposing granite mountain in front and its mysterious triangular inscription, and the birds, monkeys, and flowering trees that surrounded us. We lived in it, and owned it too. Then we left it behind, and embarked on a journey we had no idea where it would lead us, although Alan thought he did...

I confess at this moment I'm so exhausted from all this saga that I can barely recount everything we've gone through, starting from scratch, to build credit, to build credibility, and find the right connections... Fortunately, today I can say it took us a while, but we hired the right people. Although, of course, Alan gets a little jealous every time our contractor accepts my suggestions... oh, well.

So here we are, running the construction marathon again, wary of every little detail, again, ready to leave a heritage, again, our work of art on top of a mountain again. Interestingly enough, when we entered our new house for the first time today, Alan was disappointed again with the dimensions of the picture window in the living room (although, this time, there is nothing shy or modest about it, and that's a statement of fact). Thus, he asked the contractor to knock it down again, just a few pieces of plywood this time.

Et voilà, history truly repeats itself; but we are better prepared, more mature, more experienced each time. In our case, after almost 12 years of so many accomplishments (and counting), I must admit that we are still stuck in our primary war of egos, as predicted by our synastry reading in the very first days of our online relationship. Who cares if we don't believe in Astrology at all, or, for that matter, in anything, or anybody else but ourselves… or at least, that's what we like to believe (although Alan would certainly tell you that he believes in God as well).

Not a bad omen for the Jewish New Year, right?

Apocalypse, Here and Now

Honestly, I'm too perplexed to make a move anytime soon, as I don't fully understand what is going on.

Despite their crushing success in misleading the American people into believing that Hillary Clinton is our "ultimate salvation," the traditional, brilliant, indispensable *New York Times* (and no, I'm not being ironic here by any means) and other powerful media channels, in a desperate move, have just thrown down their last wild card by announcing in today's headlines Hillary's apocalyptic "Last Days" threat: "I'm the last thing standing between you and the Apocalypse."

Come on: There's no such thing as the "Apocalypse," a biblical fantasy that ran its course in our daunting "information society," something theoretically worse than the *status quo* we were left with, thanks to political incompetence. This would include ISIS, Syria, and similar "hassles."

We are living in hell, my friends, although at this moment, in a way, hell seems to be far away if you live in the U.S. At any rate, especially after Robert de Niro's latest and equally successful "basement rumblings" online, and the regrettable, manipulated publishing of Donald Trump's "sexist" remarks from 11 years ago, I was on the verge of accepting their frightening arguments and voting Trump out... until this overbearing, apocalyptic rhetoric awakened me. What was I thinking?

I'd been painfully debating with myself over the last weekend if I should stand up for or against *malekind* (yes, I know the term does not exist, I just made that up). Half or more of the males of our species distanced themselves conveniently from Trump's crude remark, "grab her by her pussy" or something. The other less than half had to confess that, although they might have uttered the contemptible words at some distant and hopefully forgotten time in their macho existences, they certainly haven't done anything remotely like it recently, and don't plan to do it ever again.

A hundred percent of dedicated husbands all over the world did their best to exhibit themselves as sensitively aloof to the outrageous invocation of feminine genitals. Except mine. A hundred percent of faithfully happy wives made a point of affirming "never my husband." Except me.

Okay. Maybe it was quite naïve of me to candidly show the world, in my about-to-be-published novel *No Degrees of Separation*, how my husband (of 12 years) and I succeeded in conquering each other's heart and soul — and why not say it, cock and cunt — through the passionate exchange of sexual conversations on the internet. In the invasive, constantly, and viciously hacked world today, imagine if we were "important" people, the kind of people who have the destiny of billions in their oft-dirty hands... Our dirty talk would certainly have fallen into mischievous, ill-intentioned minds and we would be toast.

Nonetheless, that intimate dirty talk saved our lives, by propelling our lonely, regretful, sorrowful human natures into a possible, loving future.

In the beginning, after I met him in person and actually began to share a roof with him, his masculine bluntness frequently shocked me, I must admit. Nothing much, really, just the strength of his vibration hovering in the air all over the place, his resolve, his thinking (and acting) power, something I had never felt, or witnessed before, or even expected from my previous husbands — who were maybe not "pussies," but certainly "boyish," immature males with underdeveloped maleness.

Concerning the "Trump's pussy-grab scandal," my husband tells me in his very direct way that, as he played sports during his youth, he had heard a lot of "locker room talk," another expression that had just fallen into disgrace. On my part, I heard him say the words, and write about feminine genitals several times.

In my opinion, what we truly need for the sake of our own sanity, is a complete, radical rehashing of the abandoned notions of "public" and "private."

I'm not attracted to Donald Trump as a man in any way, let me make that clear. I wouldn't let him touch my genitals at any time just because he is a "star" — albeit an unquotable one — or a billionaire, or even the potential president of the United States. These are not things I value in life, by any means, and while we're at it, I would never use them to advance any kind of plan. Yet, I deeply appreciate the way Trump is, consciously or not, highlighting the painful hypocrisies that are truly and surely killing us, taking us straight into harm's way, whether apocalyptic or not.

After all these years of feminist activism, women have now turned into ridiculous pussycats, who call so much attention to their "often abused" genitals that nothing else seems to be relevant. What happened to our beautiful sexual revolution? To free love? To girls being able to choose their sexual partners as they pleased? Much of what is said and exposed is, indeed, painful and shameful. However, a significant percentage of it is just… plain human sex as it is, man and woman in their own specie's life-preserving intercourse; and it is paramount that we highlight the difference.

Today, after the clear exposure of the "fear agenda" that is now underway at full speed — which is, in a way, a deep relief, for now we can not only feel it, but also see it and read about it — I am very angry, and fearful indeed.

Nevertheless, let me be very clear: It is not the Donald Trumps of this world whom I fear, but their opponents, the ones who are doing everything in their detrimental reach to make us weak, dependent, and sleepy.

Wake up, America. Wake up, world; and do it today, without further delay.

BUILDING IN AMERICA

Seriously, I had no intention of writing this week. I was very upset, and determined not to write about upsetting things anymore, as it made me feel even worse. After all, real life had us sufficiently on the hook.

However, this morning, our contractor awakened me abruptly at 8 o'clock... Alright, I know this sounds quite absurd, but in this dark cage where we've been living for ages now (I mean, two years), made even darker during these last days of daylight savings time, it was practically "the middle of the night."

Moreover, folks, I was dreaming. I haven't been sleeping a lot lately, not being yet completely integrated into the "Popping Pills Society of the United States of America." Which will happen, God willing, as soon as I enter my 66th year. That is, if "so and so" gets elected and decides to preserve our Social Security and Medicare, plus our human and gun-carrying rights, among so many others. As I'd heard early on in a radio show, these would include "the right to have sex and have someone impregnate you, and to demand that this person is not ugly or undesirable," and also the indisputable right to use the bathroom of your choice, or have your doctor "perform a mandatory hysterectomy" — and other scary, voluntary procedures — in case you are too tired of being a woman in this masculine world, "encouraged" to clean, to cook, to wash… in addition to make all the necessary money to support your household, and still look young and refreshed all the time. Moreover, in case you're a foreigner like me, to be able to speak perfect English, and perform like a genius in every enterprise you undertake, including building a house… Enough. Give me that envied penis of yours and shut up already.

So, I was dreaming, and in my dream, I met this writer whose book I'm now in the process of translating from Portuguese, a year later than expected. The man is a saint, or nearly so, a pilgrim who walked from Canterbury to Rome across stunning European landscapes, and valleys and mountains and ruins. Yesterday, for example, he was looking for a place to sleep late at night, as I was struggling to finish my "daily quota." I couldn't get there, and neither could he, in that particularly inspiring stretch of text. At any rate, when I met him in the dream, he was not walking, but riding a bike; and as he rushed past me, I told him in triumph, "Here it is! 25% ready at last!"

As the noisy phone rang, he was cycling away. I jumped out of bed and Alan and I drove up the hill without even indulging in a cup of coffee. The present problem is, I'm not experienced with pitched roofs, as you well know. Therefore, the day before, when I saw for the first time the recently erected roof under which I'm supposed to live for the rest of my life, I was truly surprised, and quite shocked, I must admit. It did not resemble my drawing at all.

During my precarious sleep, I had another subliminal hunch, which was about to prove itself correct as soon as we got to the construction site: Rather than the expected six clerestory windows, for unexplained reasons there were seven up there, according to my subconscious mind.

"*¡Oye! ¿Dónde están los planos?*" asked the contractor in broken Spanish.

I was ahead of him on that one, as my own broken Spanish is much better. Not only that: I had been discussing the entire matter with my Mexican framer the day before, in broken Spanglish (with a Portuguese accent), and was proud of it. But it didn't take me long to discover that this framer, was, in fact, in the service of Marcos, another Mexican contractor I would never have access to, who, for his part, responded to our American contractor — all this on cell phones, rarely or never onsite. So one minute after Rodolfo (#3 in the construction chain) and I reached an agreement about the clerestory windows and a few other crucial things, the primary bosses were talking furiously on their cell phones, each in their own national language, while my puzzled "Bauhaus-Flat-Roof" mind was having serious trouble fathoming what the heck had happened to the "adapted" South-Carolinian Craftsman design, which I intended to make "as low-pitched as possible," just enough to fool our demanding HOA.

The whole situation was going downhill, literally. Looking down the slope from the about-to-be living room picture window, one could see the steel poles — which, at some point, would sustain the floating back porch — painfully puncturing the rummaged dirt some 20-something feet below. Huge!

"Everything about this house is huge," said the American contractor, trying to convince me that the very high ceiling was completely in order.

"We could as well hang a cross on the top," said Alan, sardonically, making reference to the absurd "cathedral" height.

As the "person in charge," I had been musing most of the night over my regrettable roofing shortcomings, and had decided quietly that I would take whatever came my way, and try to adapt to it. After all, as a Brazilian flat-roofer, I didn't know the first thing about the weight of snow, or thermal requirements and window flanges, for that matter. Come on, give me some slack; I'm in desperate need of a break here.

The contractor wouldn't give up that easily. He was determined not only to have it right, but to make me "satisfied," and was fiercely working on it. The morning meeting lasted more than two hours, during which he tried insistently to convince me of what I had convinced myself already during the previous sleepless night, notwithstanding the fact that I was sound asleep and dreaming when his early call woke me up suddenly.

In the end, while I was struggling to justify myself with respect to the pitch of the roof, which had come out wrong, but right, according to my own wrong plans, he told me this:

"When I first saw your plans, I told myself this would be a tiny little house, although I managed to convince the bank that it was otherwise. However, curiously enough, when you enter the building everything feels great, majestic even: the high ceiling, the outstanding view, the huge windows and doors; everything works beautifully together. Therefore, while doing it wrong, you've done it perfectly right."

"Well, yeah. That's the very definition of art," I said, still stuck in defensive mode. "It may be unintended, done sort of blindly, but it comes out perfectly beautiful in the end."

The same will happen with our remarkable house, I

hope. Meanwhile, as we were immersed in this highly philosophical debate, searching for an aesthetic quality of life, little did we know that the internet had been hacked, and the all-fragile house of cards of our marvelous technological civilization had been falling apart for at least a couple of hours, on a good percentage of U.S. territory.

The Russians are coming, they say, to finally take you away… away… away…

A Homestretch Narrative

Honestly, I don't remember another year in which I lost so many friends.

Oh, well. Not to death, oh no, although I'm certainly getting old enough for that... but to Facebook.

It all started in my native Brazil, during a time of radical political turnover: The party in power for the last... hmm... 14 years, give or take, was proven corrupt, and worse, completely, undoubtedly unfit for office. I'm sure you don't know what I mean when I say "corruption in office," or, for that matter, "unfit for office." We were quite lucky that we preserved the country. Look what happened, or is happening, in Venezuela, for example.

Yet, Brazil was radically split, and the community in which I should fit — but I surely don't, never did — that of writers and intellectuals, was invested heavily in denying reality. They still are, which speaks volumes about the current "intelligentsia."

In the end, those enlightened minds didn't have a say, and the truth prevailed. Let me remind you that, in Brazil, it was far easier than it is here in the U.S. to spot the "ultimate" truth, as it was ultimately as obvious as our shrinking jobs, income, and infrastructure. And yet...

I don't know why, but my deepest instincts tell me, have been telling me for a while, that Brazil is a kind of "case study" — in this case, fortunately, a pretty successful one — of what is happening in a world in which the glorious left is progressively (okay, I apologize for the pun) being transformed into the "regressive left."

I've seen the term for a while, but this week I was happy to see that one of my "gurus" from a long time ago, Michael Schermer, the editor and publisher of *Skeptic Magazine*, and a *Scientific American* monthly columnist, has adopted it. I began to read the "official debunker" during a phase of my life in which I was totally and convincingly involved with the supernatural and spiritual truths; I even called myself a "shaman," go figure. Nevertheless, I kept myself healthily doubting, open to envisioning my truths as "pure myth." I suppose I always needed to have something, or someone, pushing me in the opposite direction, to avoid becoming carried away too easily, launched into the dubious realm of self-fulfilling fantasies — a task Alan performs perfectly nowadays, on a daily basis.

Therefore, this week, Schermer tweeted what he qualified as "the best one-paragraph summary of the problem with the regressive left, victim feminism, and political correctness" he had ever read, and I identified with it, thus feeling less "alone in the world" for a while. Such is the power of "sharing our thoughts."

This year, as I was saying, I lost several friends, including a few new American ones, to "victim feminism," one among many misleading ailments that have been plaguing us in this era of intense, opinionated sharing by people who, not so long ago, would never have risked making their voices heard, or spoken.

Is this good? Is this "freedom of speech"?

I don't think so.

A vast majority of these new "owners of the truth," whom we have elected and vested in public manipulation by willingly participating in social media, barely know what they're talking about. Their "line of research" is largely hearsay — wrong, or, at least, incomplete information that will, eventually, and frequently, be debunked before the end of the day. It is the perennial manipulation of the manipulators in a mental environment that is strongly biased, and changeable, and frankly, almost "incestuous." I have no idea why this word, in particular, came to mind, but it did.

Now, here in the U.S., in a brand-new opinion-exchanging environment, in which I had the rare opportunity to present myself in an entirely new and never-experienced view, as nobody here knows me, it didn't take me long to occupy the wrong camp, naturally against my obvious "intellectual" peers. In a much more dangerous domain, this time, and with much more serious consequences than in my native Brazil. After all, it is about not only the American future, but also about the future of western civilization as we've known it.

Yes, I'm talking about the 2016 American elections, in which I positioned myself in favor of Donald Trump, the horrible, disgusting, stupid, ignorant, misogynist, racist, bigoted, dishonest, tax-evading, and pussy-grabbing Donald Trump. Did I forget something? Probably.

One of my biggest, most shocking and regrettable "losses" during the present "friend-losing" season happened when I criticized one of them about his explicit adoration of Michelle Obama. He cut me off immediately, mercilessly, without even granting me a chance to explain myself. Okay, I know, I'm playing with fire here. Michelle Obama is forbidden territory, an all-acclaimed national saint, a sacred icon. But I couldn't really blame myself, because the person in question was a classic, widely-known celebrity (at least in Brazil), actively invested against the *status quo*, a social critic and an acerbic artistic beacon… who has now turned himself into a regressive leftist, as did so many of our most incensed icons. Except that he does not know it yet. As millions like him, my ex-friend firmly believes that he is on the side of the just, fighting not only for the common good, but also for the highest good. Another manipulator turned manipulated, highly praised and widely amplified by mainstream social media. What a shame.

By "voting" for Donald Trump (as you all know, I don't vote, although in the current "rigged" system I could, if I truly wanted), I keep myself on the firmer terrain of "being against." As a former feminist — not in slogans and words, but in actions — I made my way as a woman who is completely and undoubtedly independent from any man, except, maybe, in the relationship aspect, as I've been proven tremendously "square" and old-fashioned in our "brave new gender world." Now, ironically, I'm against a *status quo* that represents everything I praised when I was against the same *status quo* in my younger years.

A few weeks ago, I must admit, I was feeling truly discouraged, not by the facts, but by the "deconstructive media facts"; that is, I believed Donald Trump was an agent of change who was doing quite poorly, with his endless stock of hidden (and belated) personal scandals… but not anymore.

We have finally reached the "homestretch" week in this present electoral season, which is fortunate, as everyone seems exhausted and fed up with it. Moreover, notwithstanding some equally hidden "Brexit effect," I now know that everything we ever stand for actually has some real effect. We just happen to ignore what it's going to be.

Out of curiosity, I just wonder who, in this social adventure that is influenced more widely by "narratives" than I've ever seen (let's face it, even the term "narrative" has acquired new meaning), will in fact occupy the highest "home" in the land. Regardless of what happens in the end, I trust we will be wise enough to handle it, and change whatever does not favor us — as humans, in the longer term.

What can we do but hope, right?

Coincidentally, on a more personal note, I also find myself in a kind of "homestretch." Although I'm ignoring exactly where I'm heading, at least I now know where my home will be: in the house we're building on top of a mountain, with potentially deficient internet connections, far from this ever-madding social media crowd.

So help me God: and may God help the United States of America.

A World Worth Fighting for

Okay: As often happens to a good majority of people our age, Alan often struggles with email issues and asks for my help, whether to classify messages received by the date or sender, or to attach a file, or to include a picture in the message body. Alan, however, is not running for President of the United States, right? He has been retired for more than 10 years; he doesn't even work (although he's been working like a dog to build our house), nor does he have the chance to influence people, except perhaps me and his two adult sons. This does not mean that he's not brilliant, of course, capable of a deep understanding of what's going on, and even of forecasting what is about to happen quite accurately.

Now, in all honesty, would you like to have a President of the United States who doesn't know the first thing about emails?

Let's face it; most people are not "tech savvy" at all. They know how to "use" technology, but they don't actually "understand" it. If they have any issue with their computers or cell phones, they call the specialist.

This has rarely been the case with me. I did turn to

my webmaster for help a few times, of course. By the way, I only hired a webmaster when my company's website grew so that it became completely unmanageable by a person who did not dedicate herself to the task 24/7. KBR's website now has more than 500 pages live, figure that.

For this and other reasons, I've been following "Clinton's email issue" with great interest. I began by researching a thing called "domain," which is the second part of the email address, after the "@," and learned that Hillary's Clinton private domain for emails is "clintonemail.com." The domain was registered initially in 2009, which makes sense, as that's when Hillary was appointed Secretary of State. Then it was renewed in 2015 — which signaled that she intended to go on using it — and is alive and well today, valid until January 2017. If this does not signal "intent," I don't know what does.

The registrar data (registrar is where you *register* your domain, and you need to pay a yearly fee to keep it current) state that this domain is actually hosted by "worldnic.com." However... when you go to that site, there's a red flag that warns you that hackers may be using your computer and stealing your data. In one word: It is not safe. Wow.

True: Although alive and hosted, the "clintonemail" domain does not have a website. By the way, it was just disclosed that the Russians are *not* responsible for any hacking designed to expose Hillary, Julien Assange said so himself in an interview. In the U.S., today, people lie without a second thought, or a clear understanding of the true danger their lies may pose.

That said, we can finally move on to the next issue: the overthrow of a candidacy by inappropriate sexual behavior. Trump's? No. Anthony Weiner's.

Oh well. Who cares about this apparently recurring

pervert, right? I have no interest whatsoever in writing about him; however, he was married to Hillary Clinton's top aide, and that's how he came to play a role here: While investigating his alleged sexting with a minor, the FBI found thousands of emails pertinent to Clinton's case, and they didn't come from a ".gov" email address. Surprise!

Although, obviously, I couldn't shape-shift into a fly and land on a piece of cake to watch while fate unfolds in Hillary's private kitchen, I can envision the scene perfectly. Oh. My. God. She was so sure that this whole boring hassle was already behind her! "And now this!" she vociferates. "Stupid woman! Hideous man!"

She might be talking about her closest allies and most faithful friends; who knows? Never trust a man with "deviant" tendencies, or someone who texts you asking you to "take off your clothes and touch yourself." Unless, of course, he's your lover, and you're both single adults in a sexting world. I had done it myself a long time ago, and I must admit that, combined with other passionate elements, it had changed my life for the better. Much better: I found a husband and a faithful companion.

On the other hand, how could one possibly forget that for every email sent there is a mandatory recipient, and that those recipients have their own devices and their own way of dealing with them? Moreover, that the recipients (gender undisclosed) might have a partner with whom they share their devices, and this partner might... and so on and so forth?

That is, notwithstanding the results of these upcoming elections, we must accept a few things as indisputable facts. Of course, the president of the United States wouldn't have to deal with his email accounts personally on a daily basis... but now I not only understand, but also agree that there was indeed a potential danger in POTUS' insistence on using his own Blackberry back in 2008... and there still is; you know what I mean.

It's practical. It's fast. It's tempting. However, something tells me that we will be forced to rethink our behavior concerning the use of email, texting, and the like when dealing with sensitive information.

Like so many sensitive areas of our lives — and this would maybe, only maybe, include our sexual lives — our communication practices will soon need to revert to more traditional forms, unfortunately: the personal touch — I mean, talking and touching in person, or have you already forgotten what that is?

That said, let's move on to the last subject today. This week, in Brazil, a majority of so-called conservative officials were elected mayors around the country. It is the biggest downfall of the Worker's Party since it has first been in office, which doesn't come as any surprise, after the latest developments in the government corruption investigation.

Which left me thinking: What the heck happened to our beloved left?

Ah, the left, all that's right, and worth fighting for... Traditionally, the left had the monopoly on social justice, equality, environmental issues, and a myriad of other crucial subjects that truly matter, and must be continually examined and redefined.

They had been great about those on so many occasions, right? It is the power of the left, of the progressives, or liberals, you name it, that makes our society advance, and this has happened several times. It has happened in civil rights, women's rights, the protection of minorities. It has happened when intellectuals, artists, and writers reflected upon our lives and tried to advance our outdated concepts, making them work better for all of us; and for that they have been persecuted, misjudged, and fought, often violently, or even fatally. Those were social martyrs, and we must not forget that, ever. They fought for all of us and made our lives much better, first by dreaming, "envisioning," then by trying to make it happen — and that was always great, but bear with me for a moment. Every time the left has been invested with power, the result has been invariably disastrous. They have destroyed countries, societies, families, and even entire cultures. They have lost themselves, and through their carelessness, their lack of touch with reality, they came this close to destroying us, I mean, destroying the human race, by manipulating biology.

I wonder why: Are these not the same great people, the same revolutionary, valuable, loving people we all cherish and admire?

Yes, they are. However, have you heard that old saying, "Be careful what you wish for?" Once they're in power, and there's no significant contrary force to control them, one that can stop them from fulfilling all their "crazy" plans, from seizing the opportunity to make it happen… all those delirious dreams, those impossible feats that eventually take us forward… Then there's nobody to debate them, to reflect upon them, to erase everything that does not work, or will not work for the common good. That is, about 95% of those wondrous dreams.

When in power, the left is invested with the certainty that they are simply the best. Everything they ever come up with is a wonderful thing; they are brighter, fairer, better, more creative, and just; there is no stopping them, and the final result spells "dis-as-ter."

Think about it; name whatever social (or economic, or political) issues you can think of, and realize how many of them have been accomplished in recent times, and ultimately resulted in disaster, or soon will.

Therefore, for our own good, I believe we should vote conservative, if this does not offend us deeply or jeopardize our core principles — "conservative," of course, meaning to "conserve" what had been working for ages... Then we can generously grant the left the glorious task of continuously confronting it, in the opposition, that is.

Don't worry; there will always be enough people coming up with valuable, dreamy, incredible ideas that will, eventually, change our society for the better. This will be even more true if they are forced to fight for it, to heroically resist being destroyed for it, and thus, automatically, keep reflecting upon it, again and again. That's what the young generations are for, by the way.

Believe me, it's no good to get what you want too easily. We're most likely wired to devalue it, and given free reign, to overdo it and lose all perspective about it, more or less like drug addicts.

That's how I've lived my entire life: fighting for what I wanted, and sure as hell, it didn't seem fair to me. And yet, that's what I now believe to be the right way.

A Grain of Salt

I was about to enter the shower when Alan's face popped through the half-opened door: "President Trump is going to speak shortly."

"Is he?"

"No. I'm just practicing it," said Alan, chuckling, a radiant smile on his face.

Alan prides himself on having been the very first to consider Donald Trump as President of the United States, and he is quite right. In a time when not even the candidate had officially launched his candidacy, if I can truly remember a world in which Trump was not campaigning all over the place, Alan was already on it. He also prides himself on being the one who "invented" the concept that "a president is someone you hire to govern the country," and sure as hell he would hire Donald Trump for the job.

I doubted him, as is the norm here at home.

As you already know, I began with Jeb, but at some point, it became abundantly clear that the younger Bush candidacy was not going anywhere; therefore, I considered a change. Being a freshman in the "Republican ecosystem," I was still sort of "crawling," and did not know exactly where to go or whom to turn to after a lifetime of devoted progressivism and preaching according to Obama's creed.

Yes, that's right. I was a fervent Obamist back in 2008, and this choice not only resulted in a book that will never be translated into English — thank God — as it almost put an end to my then recent marriage to Alan.

We were in Hawaii to visit our son when Obama was first elected. Two other couples were traveling in the van that took us from the airport to the hotel; one came from Washington DC, and had cast an early vote — for Obama, of course. The other, if I'm not mistaken, was retired and living in Oregon, in a place where "most people go on holiday." The husband proceeded to affirm that, if Obama was elected, the U.S. (economy, I think he meant, but I cannot be sure) would lose at least 10 years, with which Alan agreed enthusiastically.

Not one single day has passed since in which Alan did not remind me of that conversation in the van. We were sitting in a bar in Oahu when Obama was declared the winner. We cheered; that is, I cheered — and the rest of the bar, of course. Alan, in all fairness, had tried his best a few hours before in our hotel room, "Well, hmm... he seems to be a good man"; but ultimately failed to convince himself.

To be honest, it took me a mere few weeks living in the United States to become a Republican. I had heard once before — with a fair degree of shock, I must admit — that "the true American is a Republican," said by a Brazilian cousin who had been living here since the 1980s. I refused to believe him, of course. The Democrats were the best in this world, and always would be.

Let's advance the calendar, and now we find ourselves on that awesome Tuesday in which our high expectations of failure... were never fulfilled. I was awake at two in the morning, shortly after the "tide" had changed, and had surrendered to sleep just half an hour before the State of Pennsylvania gave Trump the electoral college votes he needed to be elected President of the United States. (Don't mind me, I'm just practicing as well.)

My reasons for supporting Trump had been extensively described by the whining media this week, in a last-ditch attempt to keep their wild "narrative" alive. The so-called narrative has already begun its demise, but let me seize this last opportunity to "put my thoughts in someone else's words" for a change, because I'm too tired to repeat it in my own words once again: "Enough of elites; enough of experts; enough of the *status quo*; enough of the politically correct; enough of the liberal intelligentsia and cultural overlords with their predominant place in the media; enough of the financial wizards who brought the 2008 meltdown and stagnant incomes and jobs disappearing offshore. That, in essence, was Trump's message," wrote Roger Cohen, in his otherwise mistaken article published in *The New York Times*, just as completely wrong as his previous "certainties" against Donald Trump. Frankly, it feels deeply disgusting to realize all the extensive manipulation of the American psyche that has been accomplished during these last eight years, something I had already described in previous chronicles.

On Thursday, Alan and I were in a warehouse investigating flooring options for our new house when he asked the manager: "How do you feel about the results of these elections?"

She remained silent for a couple of minutes. Then, she seemed to measure us carefully from head to toe, before, quite hesitantly, giving a response:

"Well... Hmm... I'm very happy."

I started to laugh, and then she explained that she was afraid to express her opinion. How pathetic was that, in a country that is so proud of practicing freedom of expression in all its ramifications?

That's correct. Notwithstanding the fact that only the need to preserve the Second Amendment has been used as a talking point in the past elections (wow, I'm so glad this had also passed!), it is in fact the First Amendment that has been under attack, although most people failed to realize that. Further, this was, to say the least, one of my utmost concerns, the one that motivated me to finally choose Donald Trump — "following my husband's lead," of course.

Yes, I wrote that last line not only to please Alan a bit, as he deserves to be pampered occasionally, but also to give ammunition to those poor people who are crying in the streets, those poor spoiled millennials who were trained extensively not to cope with life's hardships, whatever they might be.

I pity them. They are so unprepared, and thus so conditioned to fail in the future. But enough of looking to the past, or we risk being transformed into pillars of salt, as, my friends, let's face it: It is a Sodom and Gomorrah of sorts that we are about to leave behind, if we speak frankly about it.

Okay, I exaggerate, as is my usual style; but you know what I mean, I guess, not in the "moralistic sense," but in the sense of real life, of the practical results of what-has-been-done. Hopefully, the future that begins today will bring the reparations we are waiting for, and we will work in this direction, trying our best to make it happen.

We were driving up the mountain on early Wednesday morning, after a practically sleepless night, when Alan turned to me and said:

"We did it, Noga."

"Yes, we did."

"Don't ever underestimate yourself. You spoke about it; you wrote about it, and you had your say. Do you know the 'precipitation principle'? The one according to which you pour growing quantities of salt into a glass of water, and they keep dissolving, until one last grain makes the salt deposit itself all at once at the bottom?"

"I do."

"You are that grain of salt."

So, this is where I leave you, my friends. This is the last chapter of this book, the last chapter of a book that seemed for quite a while to be destined for the garbage bin, as it had rooted for Donald Trump most of the time. It is the last chapter, I hope, of a book that felt so distressing so many times, when I was sure that the values it was defending were about to be engulfed by a much more powerful narrative. Even more so, by the practice of narratives that we loathed so deeply, but seemed to be impotent to fight against.

Yet it wasn't. We weren't. Our voice was heard. Our voice had also joined millions of other voices we didn't even know were out there, waiting.

There is no better occasion to repeat a widely worn-out cliché, and for that I do apologize: This is the first day of the rest of our lives.

Hurray!

Noga Sklar was born in Tiberias, Israel, in 1952. She grew up in Belo Horizonte, Brazil, and lived for 30 years in Rio de Janeiro, a city she eventually left behind to take refuge in Serenity Valley, a paradise among the mountains of Petropolis. Noga met her American husband Alan Sklar in 2004, through the American Jewish dating site, JDate. This meeting gave new impetus to her life and literary career, inspiring her first novel, *No Degree of Separation,* published in English in 2016. She now lives in Greenville, SC, where she moved with her husband in October 2014.

E-mail: noga@nogasklar.com